DBT WORKBOOK FOR TEENS

PRACTICAL <u>EXERCISES</u> TO REGULATE EMOTIONS,

COPE WITH STRESS AND DISCOVER COMMUNICATION SKILLS

ERIN PARKER

Thank you!!!

Dear Valued Reader,

I sincerely thank you for choosing the DBT Workbook for Teens.

Your decision to invest in this book is a testament to your commitment to emotional well-being and personal growth for yourself and those you care about.

This workbook is a guide designed to help you navigate the complexities of adolescence and beyond. The activities within these pages are crafted to empower you with practical tools to regulate *emotions*, manage *stress*, and enhance *communication skills*.

Your **Opinion** is invaluable in shaping the future of this work. On page 122, you can easily share your thoughts and suggestions. Your input ensures that we continue to meet the needs and interests of readers like you.

I also have a **Special Surprise** for those journeying through this workbook. Towards the end of your read, you will find a unique present as a token of my appreciation for your dedication to personal development. If curiosity gets the better of you, feel free to flip directly to page 122 to discover it. On the next page, you will find a few previews!

At the end of the book, useful **FAQS** will help you understand why this book is so valuable, why it is a tool for applying DBT principles independently without neglecting external help and much more.

Thank you once again for your trust and support. May this workbook be a stepping stone towards a healthier, happier, and more resilient you.

Warm regards,

Erin Parker

Author of "DBT Workbook for Teens"

Two Assets .... and more ...

You also have these valuable resources:

→ **Printable & Full-Colored Worksheets** (.pdf): Use fun and creativity to enhance your emotional well-being. These colorful pages make learning and applying DBT skills in your daily life fun and easy.

→ **Personal Journal**: This beautifully designed journal allows you to capture your thoughts, feelings, and progress. Reflect on your journey and monitor your progress as you work through the pages.

Why Grab These Assets?

❖ **Enhanced Learning**: The colored activities are visually appealing, making it easier to understand and remember the DBT skills.

❖ **Personal Growth**: Use the journal to reflect on your journey, set goals, and celebrate your achievements.

❖ **Stress Relief**: Writing down your thoughts can help you manage stress and emotions more effectively.

Stay motivated, stay inspired, and enjoy your path to inner peace and growth! Now, go to page 122 and discover your perks.

Table of Contents

Introduction

If you're reading this book, you're moving on an extraordinary journey of personal growth. This work has been specifically created for you, a teenager seeking tools and strategies to navigate life's challenges healthy and balanced. **Dialectical Behaviour Therapy (DBT)** is a therapeutic approach that helps you <u>better understand</u> *yourself*, your *emotions*, and your *behaviors*, providing <u>practical tools</u> to manage stress, navigate complex relationships, and overcome other issues you may encounter during your teenage years.

You are not alone on this journey of growth. Famous individuals like *Selena Gomez*, an internationally renowned pop star, and *Simone Biles*, an exceptional Olympic gymnast, have openly spoken about the importance of DBT in their lives. These testimonials demonstrate that DBT can be a powerful tool for addressing personal challenges and achieving emotional well-being.

This book will guide you through activities and reflections that will help you apply the principles of <u>DBT in your everyday life</u>. You will learn to develop self-awareness, emotion regulation, effective communication, and emotional resilience skills. It will be a journey of self-discovery, growth, and personal transformation.

Get ready to explore yourself, overcome obstacles, and achieve your goals. The journey you're embarking on will be exciting. We are here to guide you on this path, providing you with support and tools to navigate your adolescence in a <u>healthy</u>, <u>positive</u>, and <u>fulfilling way</u>.

The book was created with the best intentions: to provide an introductory path to DBT; any inaccuracies will be corrected to improve the reader's experience.

Chapter 1: The Effectiveness of DBT

THE CONCEPTS OF DBT

Dialectical Behavioural Therapy (DBT) is a therapeutic approach that combines the Oriental wisdom of mindfulness with practical skills for emotion management, effective communication, and distress tolerance. *Dr Marsha M. Linehan*, a pioneer in cognitive-behavioral therapy, developed DBT. It is a form of cognitive-behavioral therapy that focuses on "acceptance" of uncomfortable thoughts and behaviors rather than struggling against them. The underlying idea is that such behaviors can be changed after being validated.

DBT is rooted in a deep understanding of the challenges teenagers face during adolescence, a transitional phase that can be turbulent and complex. This therapy offers specific tools to effectively address emotional and relational challenges, helping you build a more balanced and fulfilling life.

DBT helps individuals who struggle with emotional and behavioral control.

Key Skills of DBT:

✓ **Mindfulness** is the ability to be fully present in the current moment without judging our experiences. Through mindfulness, you will develop greater self-awareness and accept your emotions without judgment. You will learn mindfulness techniques to experience the power of awareness and focus in the here and now.

✓ **Emotion Regulation**: during adolescence, emotions can feel overwhelming and unpredictable. Emotion regulation provides tools to recognize, understand, and manage your feelings healthily and constructively. You can identify warning signs of intense emotions, develop relaxation strategies, and replace negative thoughts with more realistic and positive ones.

✓ **Effective Communication**: Interpersonal relationships can be complex and conflictual at this stage of life. You will learn assertive communication and conflict resolution skills to express your thoughts and feelings clearly and respectfully. You can also empathetically listen to others and find satisfying solutions for all parties involved.

✓ **Distress Tolerance**: you may experience stressful or challenging situations. Distress tolerance provides you with strategies to navigate these situations healthily and constructively. You will practice <u>stress management</u>, engage in pleasant distractions, and practice <u>self-soothing</u> to overcome difficult moments with resilience.

DBT is supported by research and studies that have demonstrated its effectiveness in improving emotion management, interpersonal relationships, and the emotional well-being of teenagers. It is a journey of personal transformation that offers you concrete tools to navigate the <u>challenges of adolescence</u> and build a more authentic life.

Get ready to discover the power of <u>awareness</u> and step aboard on your journey toward a more balanced and empathetic life. Put in some effort because DBT can open new doors and transform your life in ways you never imagined.

TRANSITION AND INSTABILITY

Adolescence is a period of significant transitions and instability, where many challenges and changes can considerably impact one's life. It is a phase of growth, discovery, and identity formation but can also be accompanied by anxiety, confusion, and emotional instability.

During this time, you may experience physical, hormonal, and social changes that can affect your emotional well-being and ability to handle daily challenges. Social pressure, family expectations, and educational challenges can create significant stress.

DBT recognizes the uniqueness of this transitional phase and provides <u>specific tools</u> to help you navigate these changes effectively. By learning practical skills, you will develop greater self-awareness, emotional understanding, and the ability to handle complex situations healthily and constructively.

You may experience a range of <u>everyday challenges</u>, including:

➢ **Evolving Identity**: you are starting to explore and define your identity. Feeling confused or uncertain about who you are and what you want to become is normal. DBT will help you develop <u>self-awareness</u>, explore your <u>values</u>, and build a solid foundation for your <u>evolving identity</u>.

➢ **Emotional Fluctuations**: emotions can be intense and unpredictable. You may shift from moments of happiness and excitement to periods of sadness and anger. This therapy will give you tools to recognize and <u>regulate your emotions healthily</u>, allowing you to develop excellent emotional stability.

➢ **Complex Interpersonal Relationships**: relationships with friends, family, and peers can become complex and conflictual. You may feel insecure in relationships or need help communicating effectively. You will learn communication and <u>conflict-resolution skills</u> to cultivate healthy and satisfying relationships.

➢ **External Pressures**: you will often experience a range of external pressures, such as educational challenges, family expectations, and the need to conform to social standards. DBT will equip you with tools to <u>manage stress</u> and healthily navigate these pressures.

Chapter 2: Awareness of the Present

LIVE THE PRESENT WITH MINDFULNESS

Mindfulness is a fundamental skill that allows us to be <u>present and aware</u> of what is happening in the current moment. It is a way of living awake, with eyes wide open, freeing ourselves from the routine and habit of living according to present patterns. It is like opening a window in our minds and letting the light of the present flow in.

When we practice Mindfulness, we intentionally focus on the <u>present moment</u> <u>without judging</u> or rejecting what is happening. It is a way of effectively observing, describing, and engaging with reality at the moment.

When we are mindful, we free ourselves from the conditioning of the past and worries about the future. We are free to enjoy life's joys and challenges fully. It feels like immersing ourselves in a river, feeling the water flow between our fingers, sensing every little sensation, and surrendering to the current without resistance.

Growing in Mindfulness requires commitment and consistent practice. It is like training a muscle, in this case, the power of the mind, to become increasingly skilled in being present and aware. Here are some fundamental **mindfulness skills** you can develop:

❖ **Non-judgmental observation**: observe your thoughts, emotions, and physical sensations without judgment. Notice what is happening within you without labelling anything as "good" or "bad." Let everything be as it is without trying to change or control it.

❖ **Accurate describing**: try to describe what you are experiencing in the present moment accurately. Use specific words to identify your emotions, thoughts, and physical sensations. This will help you develop greater awareness of your internal experiences.

❖ **Active participation**: fully immerse yourself in the experience of the present moment. Be actively engaged in what you do, whether eating, walking, or conversing. Notice the details, smells, sounds, and physical sensations surrounding you. Be present and involved in the here and now.

❖ **Sustained focus**: concentration is a key skill for developing Mindfulness. Practice staying focused on your actions without getting distracted by thoughts or external factors. When the mind wanders, gently bring it back to the present and the task.

❖ **Cultivating patience**: Mindfulness requires patience and kindness towards yourself. Don't expect to become an immediate master of Mindfulness. It is a gradual process that takes time and practice. Embrace every moment of training as an opportunity for growth and learning.

Mindfulness skills are the specific behaviors we can practice to cultivate this awareness. *Meditation*, for example, is a form of mindfulness practice where we focus on our mind, body sensations, emotions, or breath. It helps us cultivate the ability to focus or open the mind. Mindfulness is also a mental state we can develop in every moment of our day. We can bring mindful attention to our breath while walking, the sensations in our body during physical exercise, or our mind while engaging in daily activities.

The beauty of Mindfulness lies in its simplicity. It does not require special tools or isolated places. We can practice it wherever we are, at any time. It is like a superpower that resides within us and can be activated anytime.

Applying Mindfulness to the management of emotions and thoughts is crucial. It allows us to <u>take control of our mind</u> rather than allowing the mind to control us. We are often unaware of our feelings, why we get angry, or our goals.

This practice helps us improve our ability to *concentrate*, develop an *open mind*, become *self-aware*, have better *stress management skills*, and navigate *intense emotions*. It provides an internal compass that guides our lives, enabling us to make more conscious decisions and live in harmony with ourselves and the world around us.
Mindfulness can become a valuable guide in your life. It helps you make more conscious decisions, better understand yourself and others, and live authentically and with fulfilment. Harness the power of Mindfulness to connect with your true self and fully embrace the present moment.

Take the time to explore these fundamental skills. Remember that every small step you take toward greater Mindfulness is a step toward a richer and more meaningful life. Whether sitting, walking, or engaged in daily activity, be present and thoroughly enjoy each moment. Mindfulness awaits you, ready to enrich your life.

R+E=W

Wise Mind (W) is a powerful resource that we all possess. It represents the harmony between Reason (R) and Emotion (E), opening the door to a deep understanding of ourselves and our world.

Imagine your Wise Mind as a bridge between your rational mind, the **Reasonable Mind**, and your emotional mind, the **Emotional Mind**. When these two forces merge, creating a mental state called **Wise Mind** allows you to see things with clarity and wisdom.

Wise Mind is where we embrace logical information and emotional experiences. It is not just a sum of the two but something deeper and integrated. It is like an inner lighthouse that illuminates the path, guiding you through life's challenges and decisions.

When you are in Wise Mind, you can integrate opposites. You are no longer stuck in rigidly rational thinking or swept away by a flood of emotions. You can recognize that there are multiple valid viewpoints and that each individual has a unique story. We understand that change is a constant in life and that seemingly opposing things can coexist. It is a way of being that connects you with your inner wisdom and helps you navigate life's turbulent waters. This mental state allows you to make wise decisions based on the awareness of that moment without passing judgment. Dialectics become a guide for us, opening us to new ways of seeing and solving problems.

Wise Mind helps you make informed decisions based on awareness of your values, emotions, and needs, balancing rationality and empathy and enabling effective communication with others.

Remember that it is a continuous journey and requires consistent practice. Over time, you will find that Wise Mind becomes a valuable companion, offering guidance and wisdom at every step of your path.

_____
_____
_____
_____
_____
_____
_____
_____
_____
_____
_____
_____
_____
_____

EXERCISE 1:
Analyse the Maze of Thought

15 mins

Objective: develop the ability to use rational thinking to solve problems and make decisions based on facts and logic. Duration: approximately 15-20 minutes.

START

1

Carefully examine the maze and observe the paths, intersections, and obstacles present. Imagine that the labyrinth represents a problem or decision that you need to face in your life.

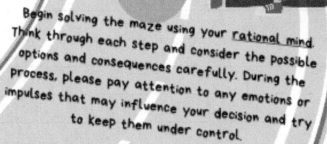

2

Begin solving the maze using your rational mind. Think through each step and consider the possible options and consequences carefully. During the process, please pay attention to any emotions or impulses that may influence your decision and try to keep them under control.

3

Write down your thoughts, strategies, and reasoning as you navigate the maze. Record your observations and reflections along the way.

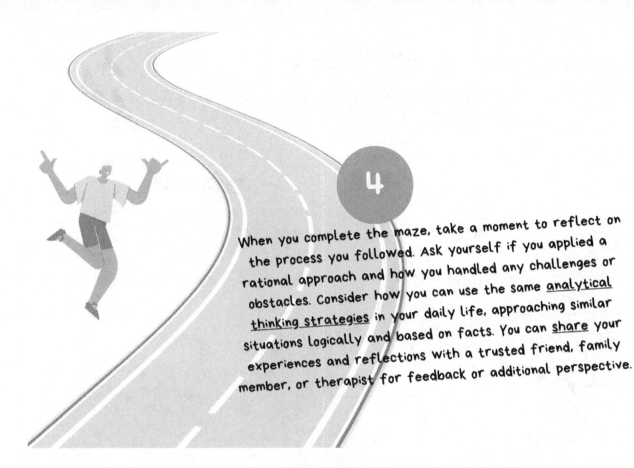

When you complete the maze, take a moment to reflect on the process you followed. Ask yourself if you applied a rational approach and how you handled any challenges or obstacles. Consider how you can use the same _analytical thinking strategies_ in your daily life, approaching similar situations logically and based on facts. You can _share_ your experiences and reflections with a trusted friend, family member, or therapist for feedback or additional perspective.

REMEMBER

that rational thinking requires practice and awareness. This exercise aims to develop your ability to _assess situations objectively_, considering the available information and making informed decisions. Good luck!

EXERCISE 2:
Colour Your Emotions

⏱ 15 mins

START HERE

1

Observe your current emotional state: "How am I feeling right now? What emotions am I experiencing?" Allow the emotions to arise without judgment.

2

Choose a colour or combination of colours that represent your current emotions. For example, you may associate blue with sadness, red with irritation, or green with calmness. Interpret the colours as you wish, based on your meaning of the emotions.

3

Using the available materials, begin creating an artwork that expresses your emotions. You can paint, draw, or create a collage. Let your feelings guide your artistic choices, allowing the emotional mind to flow through your creations.

4

During the creative process, reflect on your emotions. Observe how they change over time and how they manifest on your canvas. Ask yourself, "What am I learning about my emotions? How can I authentically express what I feel?"

5

Once the artwork is complete, observe it. Notice how your emotions have been transformed into a visual expression. Describe what you have discovered about your feelings through this artistic expression.

6

Finally, take a moment to write down your reflections on your experience. Describe the emotions you explored, the sensations you felt during the artistic process, and your discoveries about your emotional mind.

This exercise allows you to explore and <u>understand your emotions through art</u>. It helps you connect with your emotional mind, creatively express your feelings, and gain greater awareness of your emotions. Remember that there are no right or wrongs in your artistic process. Let your <u>emotional mind</u> guide your creativity and enjoy the explorative journey within your emotions.

_____
_____
_____
_____
_____
_____
_____
_____
_____

EXERCISE 3:

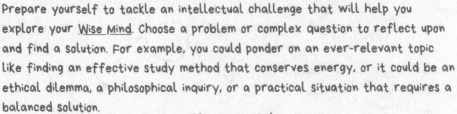
Study Method

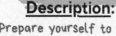

Description:

Prepare yourself to tackle an intellectual challenge that will help you explore your Wise Mind. Choose a problem or complex question to reflect upon and find a solution. For example, you could ponder on an ever-relevant topic like finding an effective study method that conserves energy, or it could be an ethical dilemma, a philosophical inquiry, or a practical situation that requires a balanced solution.

Actions You Can Take

Gather all relevant

01 information and analyse possible perspectives and solutions. Reflect on your past experiences, values, and inner wisdom. Write a list of pros and cons for each possible answer.

Use your Wise Mind

02 to find a balanced and reasonable solution. Write down your thoughts, reasoning, and the solution you have chosen.

Reflect on the

03 decision-making process and the effectiveness of your Wise Mind in finding a balanced solution.

This exercise aims to

04 help you develop your critical, analytical, and reflective thinking skills by encouraging access to your Wise Mind.

You will experience

05 the power of making decisions based on inner wisdom and finding a balance between your emotions and rational thinking.

Remember, the goal of the exercise is to stimulate reflection and the application of the Wise Mind in the decision-making process, so tailor the workout according to your interests.

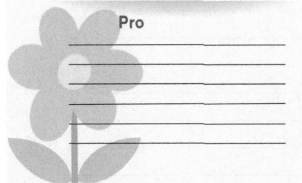

Pro

_____
_____
_____
_____

Cons

_____
_____
_____
_____

EMBRACE THE MOMENT

The capacity for **observation** is an essential element of mindfulness and plays a fundamental role in adolescents' practice of DBT. Observing means consciously paying attention to the <u>present moment</u> without judgment or immediate reaction. This allows us to connect more deeply with ourselves and our environment.

- ✦ **Observe without words.** Set aside words for a moment and fully immerse yourself in the present. Become aware of what is happening around and within you without describing it in words. Be present, allowing your senses to capture every detail of the experience.

- ✦ **Open the five senses.** Observation involves directing attention both inward and outward. Using the five senses (sight, hearing, smell, taste, and touch), we can tune into sensory experiences and entirely perceive our environment. We can observe the physical sensations in our body, the emotions that arise and dissolve, the sounds that surround us, and the smells and tastes we encounter. Through this sensory openness, we deepen our connection with the immediate experience.

- ✦ **Welcome and let go.** Observation teaches us to welcome the experience, including thoughts, emotions, and sensations, without seeking to change or control it. We neither cling to an experience nor push it away. Observe with kindness and let everything pass through you without trying to control or hold onto anything. This openness and acceptance help us manage emotional challenges more flexibly and adapt better.

- ✦ **Awareness of thoughts and emotions.** In observation, we learn to recognize that thoughts and emotions are events that manifest and dissolve in our consciousness. We can observe them as phenomena in motion rather than fully identifying with them. Experience the flow and change, acknowledging that you are more than what you think or feel at any moment. This awareness allows us to develop a healthy distance from our thoughts and emotions, avoiding being overwhelmed.

- ✦ **Observe without judgment.** Non-judgmental observation involves an open and unbiased mind. We do not judge our experiences as right or wrong, positive or negative, but accept them as they are without condemning them.

- ✦ **Practice non-judgmental acceptance of what arises in your awareness.** Let each experience be as it is, without labelling it as good or bad, right or wrong. Free yourself from the tendency to evaluate and criticize, creating space for a broader, more compassionate understanding. Be a neutral observer, welcoming every aspect of the experience with kindness and curiosity.

Explore the skill of observation every day, allowing this practice to enrich your awareness and improve your relationship with yourself and others.

_____

_____

_____

EXERCISE 4:
Body Talks

Objective:

develop awareness of body sensations through complete immersion in the five senses.

STEP 1

Find a quiet and relaxing place where you can sit comfortably. Close your eyes and take a few deep breaths to centre and relax. Bring your attention to your body and take note of the sensations you perceive at this moment.

STEP 2

Now, focus on the sense of sight. Imagine opening your eyes and finding yourself in a particular place. Visualize the details of this place in your mind. Observe the colours, shapes, light, and shadow. Notice how these images make you feel if they evoke specific emotions or thoughts.

STEP 3

Move on to the sense of hearing. Imagine being able to hear the sounds of your imaginary environment. Be aware of the sounds that surround you, both near and far. Take note of the tones, rhythms, and various sound nuances. Also, listen to the internal sounds of your body, such as the heartbeat or the sound of your breath.

STEP 4

Next, shift your attention to the sense of touch. Imagine feeling the sensation of different surfaces or temperatures on your skin. Be aware of the pleasant and unpleasant tactile sensations in your imagination. Reflect on the feelings that influence your emotional state and your thoughts.

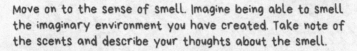

STEP 5

Move on to the sense of smell. Imagine being able to smell the imaginary environment you have created. Take note of the scents and describe your thoughts about the smell.

STEP 6

Finally, it's time to focus on the sense of taste. Imagine tasting a food or a drink. What flavours emerge in your mouth? What aromas do they remind you of? Take note of any thoughts or associations that arise from these sensations.

STEP 7

After exploring each sense, take a moment to reflect on your observations. What did you notice through your sensory imagination? Were there any specific thoughts, emotions, or reactions that you experienced?

How do you feel now compared to before?

Are there any sensations or thoughts that you would like to delve into or explore further?

When you're ready, slowly open your eyes and carry this awareness of your body sensations throughout your day.

Your Goal: Note: You can repeat this exercise regularly to develop a greater awareness of your body sensations through sensory imagination.

_____

_____

_____

_____

_____

_____

EXERCISE 5:
Matter of Perspective

OBJECTIVE:

Develop observation skills through mindful exploration of colours in the surrounding environment. - Sit comfortably. Take a few deep breaths to relax and focus on the present moment.

01
DIRECT YOUR ATTENTION

to the colours around you. Observe objects, surfaces, plants, and surrounding elements. Notice the shades and intensity of the colours. Observe how they change based on light, shadow, or distance. You can focus on a single object or explore the panorama around you.

02
NOW, SELECT A COLOUR

that attracts you more than the others. It could be the sky's blue, the green of leaves, or any other colour that inspires you. Focus on this colour and let yourself be entirely enveloped by its presence.

03
TAKE NOTE OF THE

details and nuances that may vary from one object to another. You can also experiment with your imagination and visualize how it would be if everything around you were that colour.

04
ALLOW YOUR EMOTIONS

and sensations to blend with the observation. Experience how different colours can influence your mood or inner reactions.

05

REFLECT ON THIS

experience. Did you notice anything new or surprising in the colours around you? How did this mindful observation of colours make you feel? Can you apply this awareness of colours in other situations in your daily life?

06

TAKE A FEW MOMENTS

to walk or move in your surrounding environment, keeping your attention on the colours you encounter. Explore this colourful world with curiosity and an open mind.

NOTE:

You can repeat this exercise in different places and times of the day to discover new shades and details in the colours around you. Mindful exploration of colours can enrich your observation skills and offer you a unique perspective on the beauty and variety of the landscape.

EXERCISE 6:

Speechless

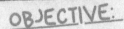

OBJECTIVE:

develop the ability to observe thoughts without judgment and stay present in the moment creatively and originally.

01 Take a sheet of paper

and colour pens and start representing your thoughts in drawings. Let your hand move freely on the page, shaping the images that emerge from your mind. You don't need to be an expert artist; expressing what you observe visually is important.

02 After completing the drawing

of your thoughts, take a moment to observe the artwork you have created. Notice the colours, shapes, and lines you used to represent your thoughts.

03 Reflect on the drawing and your

experience. Describe your emotions or sensations when observing your thoughts visualized in an illustration. Did you notice something that would have escaped if you had represented your thoughts verbally?

04 Remember that you can repeat

this exercise whenever you want to cultivate the ability to observe your thoughts without judgment and in a creative way. Experience transforming your ideas into art and discover how this practice influences your understanding of yourself.

Note:

This exercise encourages creative expression as a means to observe and understand your thoughts without the use of words. You can personalize the exercise using other materials or techniques, such as watercolours or collages, to make your experience more unique and meaningful. The important thing is to embrace the creative aspect of observing your thoughts, discovering new ways to express yourself.

_____

_____

_____

_____

_____

_____

_____

_____

_____

_____

_____

_____

_____

_____

_____

THE STORYTELLER OF YOURSELF

Describing what we observe allows us to become narrators of our experiences. Through the description capacity, we can give meaning to our sensations, emotions, and thoughts by describing what we are experiencing. This skill helps us better understand ourselves and communicate effectively with others.

We should focus on concrete and objective information when practising description, avoiding adding interpretations or personal judgments. Description allows us to distinguish what is happening from how we interpret it, enabling us to see things as they are.

We are attentive witnesses to our experiences. Let's explore how we can utilize the capacity for description in our mindfulness practice:

★ **Describing physical sensations**: Take a moment to notice the physical sensations you experience. You can tell the temperature of your skin, the feeling of breath entering and exiting, or the feeling of contact between your feet and the floor.

★ **Describing emotions**: Become aware of the feelings that arise within you. You can use words like "joy," "sadness," "anger," or "fear" to describe them. Also, take note of the nuances and intensities of emotions, such as "a gentle feeling of happiness" or "a strong sense of frustration."

★ **Describing thoughts**: Observe your thoughts as they arise in your mind. Try to put them into words without judging or evaluating them. For example, you can say, "The thought of taking a walk crosses my mind," "I'm reflecting on a school assignment," or "I have the thought that someone might judge me."

⊙ **Describing the surrounding environment**: Focus your attention on the surrounding environment. Describe what you see, hear, smell, and touch. Take note of the colours, sounds, smells, or textures of objects around you. Be detailed and specific in your words.

_____

_____

_____

_____

_____

_____

_____

_____

_____

_____

_____

EXERCISE 7:
Words Matter

Objective:
Foster awareness of using words and the ability to express one's experiences accurately.

1

WORDS INFLUENCE YOUR EXPERIENCES

and relationships with others. Choose a recent situation you have experienced and would like to explore through the description. It can be a moment of joy, frustration, sadness, or other emotion.

2

TAKE A MOMENT TO

observe what you have experienced in that situation carefully. Notice the physical sensations, emotions, thoughts, and aspects of the surrounding environment that characterized that experience.

3

NOW, BEGIN TO DESCRIBE

that situation using precise and meaningful words. Do your best to convey with words what you have observed and experienced without giving personal judgments or interpretations.

At the end of the exercise, take a moment to notice how you feel. Using precise and meaningful words to describe your experiences can increase awareness and more effective communication.

MIND MAP

_____

_____

_____

_____

_____

4

FOCUS ON THE POWER OF

words. Which words can more accurately capture your sensations, emotions, and thoughts? How can you make your description more vibrant and engaging?

5

LET THE WORDS FLOW

freely without trying to modify or judge them. The goal is to create an authentic and meaningful description. Reread what you have written. What have you learned about yourself through this description? What nuances and details have you noticed, thanks to your chosen words?

6

IF YOU FEEL COMFORTABLE

share your description with someone you trust. You can discuss the effect words have had on understanding the experience.

EXERCISE 8:
Scavenger Hunt

Description: in this exercise, I invite you to go on a scavenger hunt where you will search for specific objects and situations that will help you develop your descriptive and observational skills.

GRAB PAPER AND PEN AND
01
list items or situations you want to observe and describe. For example, you could include a flower, an interesting sound, an architectural detail, or a pleasant scent. Try to include a variety of sensory categories in this list, such as sight, hearing, touch, taste, and smell.

GO TO A PARK OR
a quiet location and explore the environment attentively. Take a walk and open up your senses.
02

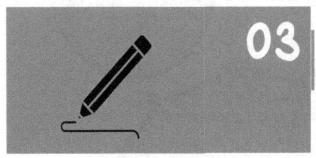
03

WHEN YOU COME ACROSS
an item or situation on your list, stop and observe it closely. Please take note of its characteristics, the details that strike you, and the sensations it evokes. Try to be as specific as possible in your description.

ONCE YOU HAVE
completed the description of an item, continue your exploration and search for the other elements on your list.
04

05

AT THE END OF THE SCAVENGER hunt, take some time to reflect on your observations and sensations. In a journal, you can write about your experiences and any thoughts that emerged during the exercise.

RECOMMENDATIONS:

Open yourself up to curiosity and be open to surprises. Notice even the small things that usually go unnoticed. Don't force your observations but let yourself be guided by the moment's spontaneity.

06

07

IF POSSIBLE

involve a friend or a group of friends in the exercise so you can share experiences and descriptions.

This exercise aims to develop your descriptive skills, observation skills, and connection with the surrounding environment. The scavenger hunt will help you cultivate greater present-moment awareness and appreciate the small wonders surrounding you.

_____
_____
_____
_____
_____
_____
_____
_____
_____

EXERCISE 9:

Just the Facts - Quiz

QUIZ TIME?

10 mins

<u>Description</u>: the quiz will test your ability to distinguish between objective facts and personal interpretations. Get ready to challenge yourself and see how well you can objectively describe the things around you!

Instructions:
★ Carefully read each question and the three answer options.
★ Select the option corresponding to an objective fact, a measurable, observable, or verifiable characteristic.
★ Answer all the questions.

After the space for comments, you will find the key to knowing the correct answers. And please, no cheating!

1 Which of the following descriptions is based on an objective fact?
a) This flower is red.
b) This flower is beautiful!
c) This flower smells like vanilla.

2 Which is an example of a description based on an objective fact?
a) This book is fascinating!
b) This book has 200 pages.
c) This book has a colourful cover.

3 Which of the following statements is an objective fact?
a) This building is impressive!
b) This building has 30 floors.
c) This building has a modern style.

4 What is a description based on an objective fact?
a) This cake is delicious!
b) This cake is trendy.
c) This cake has a layer of chocolate.

5 Which of the following statements is an objective fact?
a) This is a luxury car!
b) This car has a 300-horsepower engine.
c) This car has a lovely colour.

 Answers at page 122

A FULL IMMERSION

The ability to **Participate** is one of the fundamental skills of Mindfulness. This competence will help you fully enter the present moment and experience your challenges.

Participating means truly "*getting in the zone*" and engaging in what you are doing. It is essential to focus entirely on the activity during your daily activities, such as dancing, cleaning, studying, or even when you feel sad. Don't worry about what happened yesterday or what might happen tomorrow. Become one with your experience, immersing yourself completely in it.

This type of participation allows you to live fully in the present moment without judging yourself or what is happening around you. Let go of distractions and worries, fully immersing your mind in the activity you are engaged in. In this state of participation, you may discover a new dimension of connection with yourself and the world around you.

During the exercises proposed below, we challenge you to choose an activity that fascinates and engages your senses. It can be something like listening to your favourite music, observing a work of art, savouring your favourite food, or even walking in nature. Choose what excites you the most and allows you to enter the participation zone fully.

As you engage in this activity, allow yourself to experience all the emotions that arise, even the negative ones. Embrace emotional challenges as part of the journey and use your Wise Mind to guide your actions instead of being overwhelmed by impulses. Through this full participation, you will develop a greater awareness of your emotions and be able to make wise and conscious decisions.

Participation is an art that requires practice and dedication, but it is worth it. When you fully immerse yourself in inspiring activities, you will discover a deep joy and connection with yourself and the world around you. You will become an active protagonist in your life, bringing greater awareness and gratitude to everything you do.

We challenge you to embrace the art of participation as a way to live every moment fully. Test yourself and fully engage in your daily activities, allowing yourself to be carried by the present energy. Experience empathy, creativity, and connection from full and conscious participation.

Actively engage in your life experience. Get involved, face challenges, and enjoy the pleasures that the present moment has to offer. Remember that every moment is an opportunity to live fully, becoming one with your actions and bringing greater awareness and happiness.

_____

_____

_____

_____

_____

_____

_____

EXERCISE 10:

Dance Again

15 mins

This exercise invites you to explore your body and senses through movement and Mindfulness of the present moment. Use dance to connect with yourself and experience a deep connection with your body and emotions.

Choose a piece of music that inspires you and makes you emotionally engaged. Find a quiet and safe space where you can move freely without interference. Start the music and begin to move to the rhythm of the melody. Allow your body to express itself freely, without judgment or concern for outward appearance.

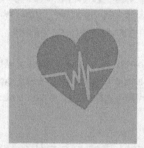

Focus on the physical sensations you experience while dancing. Notice the tension and relaxation of your muscles, the fast or calm heartbeat, the feel of the floor beneath your feet, and any other sensations that arise. Also, pay attention to your emotions. Observe how they manifest in your body as you dance. Can you feel joy, sadness, anger, or other emotions? Allow these emotions to be expressed through your movement.

Describe to yourself the physical sensations and emotions you are experiencing. Use words to label them and bring them into awareness. Continue to dance and explore your body for at least 10 minutes. Keep your attention focused on the present moment, the sensations, and the emotions that arise during the dance. When you are finished, please take a few moments to sit or lie down in silence, observing the residual sensations in your body and allowing them to fade away slowly.

You can also experience dancing in pairs or groups, sharing the experience with others. Remember to respect your limits and listen to your body during the exercise. Modify the movements according to your needs and sensations.

If you feel comfortable, you can write about your experiences and observations during the exercise. This can strengthen your awareness and reflect on your personal growth experiences.

_____

_____

_____

_____

_____

_____

_____

_____

_____

_____

_____

_____

_____

_____

_____

_____

_____

_____

EXERCISE 11:
Wise Mind ON

<u>Description</u>: In this exercise, we will integrate the concepts of Wise Mind and Mindful Participation through sports activity. By experiencing active and mindful participation in sports, we can develop our ability to be present in the moment and fully engage in the practice of sports.

1 Choose a sport that you are passionate about or want to explore. It could be soccer, basketball, dance, swimming, or any other sport that fascinates you. Take a moment to prepare for the sports activity mentally. Take deep breaths and focus on your breath, letting go of distractions and anchoring yourself in the present moment.

2 Begin the sports activity with the awareness of fully participating. Focus on the physical sensations you experience while engaging in the sport. Notice the sensations in your body, movements, sounds around you, and interaction with other participants.

3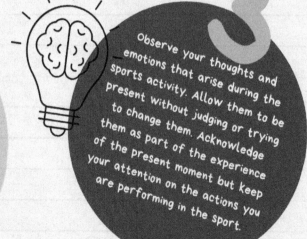
Observe your thoughts and emotions that arise during the sports activity. Allow them to be present without judging or trying to change them. Acknowledge them as part of the experience of the present moment but keep your attention on the actions you are performing in the sport.

4 Fully experience the emotions that arise during the sports activity. If you feel frustration from a mistake or enthusiasm from a success, allow these emotions to be present without suppressing or identifying with them. Be aware of how emotions influence your attitude and performance in sports.

5

Stay focused on the present throughout the entire sports practice. Avoid letting your mind wander to thoughts about the past or future. Direct your awareness to your actions in the present moment and fully enjoy the experience of the sport.

6

At the end of the sports activity, take a moment to reflect on how you felt during the process of mindful participation in sports. What have you learned about yourself? What have you noticed about your ability to be present in the moment while engaging in sports? Consider how you can bring this Mindfulness into sports and your daily life.

TIPS

Tips for parents or teachers:
Encourage teenagers to choose a sport that excites and stimulates them. It is also important to emphasize the significance of being present at the moment during sports practice and allowing emotions and thoughts to arise without judgment. Support teenagers in the process of reflecting on and integrating the practice of mindful participation in sports into their daily lives.

EXERCISE 12:
Connected with the World

10 mins

This exercise will focus on mindful participation through connecting with the objects around us. By experiencing a sense of connection and harmony with the elements, we can develop a greater awareness of our relationship with the external world.

1 Choose an object or surface to connect with, such as the floor, a chair, a blanket, or any other object that draws your attention. Ensure that you are in a quiet and safe environment.

2 ...ct your attention to where your ...dy touches that object or surface. ...example, if you choose the floor, notice the sensation of your feet touching the floor.

3 Reflect on the harmony of the object or surface at the point of contact. Consider how that object supports you, provides you with a foundation, or a path to reach other things. Reflect that the object or surface does not let you fall.

4 Experience touching that object surface and focus on this gentle connection. Observe the tactile sensations, texture, temperature, and other characteristics you can perceive through contact.

Cultivate a sense of connection, love, or care towards that object or surface. Imagine that the thing embraces you, surrounds you, or provides security. Feel gratitude for the interaction with that object or surface.

Notice how your mental state changes during this exercise. You may feel a sense of calm, appreciation, or a deeper connection with the environment that surrounds you.

You can repeat this exercise with different objects or surfaces, exploring the unique connections and kindness that each of them offers.

_____
_____
_____
_____
_____
_____
_____
_____
_____
_____
_____
_____

OBSERVE AND ACCEPT

No Judgment

A crucial element in developing Mindfulness is the ability to **observe without judgment**. This means noticing what is happening around us without labelling it as good or bad. We focus on the observable facts of the situation, relying solely on what we can perceive through our senses.

When we observe without judgment, we recognize what is harmful or helpful, but we avoid making moral judgments. It is essential to understand that we cannot live without making judgments. However, we aim to become aware of our decisions and replace them with objective descriptions. In doing so, we gain greater control over our emotions and reactions.

When we realize that we have made a judgment, it is important not to judge our decision. Instead, we kindly accept this recognition and remind ourselves that our goal is non-judgmental awareness. By practising this skill, we can develop an <u>open mind</u> and <u>greater tolerance</u> towards others and ourselves.

Parents or teachers should encourage teenagers to practice non-judgmental observation daily, helping them develop a more compassionate and accepting mindset.

Share personal experiences on how non-judgmental observation has benefited you in certain situations.

Remember that the ability to observe without judgment is a significant step in building a solid foundation for a mindful and resilient mind.

_____
_____
_____
_____
_____
_____
_____
_____
_____
_____
_____

EXERCISE 13:

Discovering the Facts

1 Think of a recent episode you have experienced, such as a car accident, a discussion with a friend, or a school trip. Choose something that lets you reflect on the events and your reactions objectively.

2 Take a moment to recall the details of that episode. Fill your mind with those moments, images, and sensations.

Objective:

_Develop the ability to observe without judgment by describing the objective facts of a recent personal experience.

3 Now, focus your attention solely on the objective facts of that episode. Describe what you saw, heard, touched, and did. Avoid giving judgments or personal interpretations.

4 Start by describing the external aspects of the episode. What did you see? What did you hear? How did you physically react? Provide specific and objective details, avoiding subjective interpretations.

5 Then, move on to describe your feelings and emotions during that episode. How did you feel at that moment? What sensations did you experience in your body? Recognize and accept the feelings without judging them as right or wrong.

Finally, reflect on your actions and behaviour during that episode. How did you respond? What did you do? Describe your actions objectively without condemning or praising yourself.

After completing the episode description, take a moment to reflect on your non-judgmental observation approach. Observe how this practice can help you better understand the events and your reactions without being influenced by biases or evaluations.

Consistently practising the description of objective facts from personal episodes helps develop an open mind and focused attention to details, reducing the impulse to judge and allowing for a more balanced view of situations.

You can repeat this exercise with different recent episodes, expanding your ability to observe without judgment and gaining a clearer perspective on your experiences. Consider keeping a journal with objective descriptions of the episodes you have experienced, encouraging the practice of non-judgmental observation in various contexts.

With the assistance of a teacher, you could organize sharing sessions where teenagers can narrate their episodes and their objective descriptions, creating a supportive environment of understanding.

It is essential to accept emotions without judgment, recognizing them as a normal part of the human experience.

_____

_____

_____

_____

_____

_____

10 mins

EXERCISE 14:
Storyteller

1

Inspired by the iconic scene from the movie "Forrest Gump," this exercise invites teenagers to become storytellers of their own lives. Imagining themselves sitting on a bench, waiting for the bus, they are encouraged to narrate an event or occurrence from their day to an imaginary person. However, describing the event objectively and without personal judgments is crucial.

2

This exercise aims to promote awareness of non-judgment and replace such judgments with an objective description of the facts. Teenagers are invited to reflect on the power of words and experience the impact of communication-based on the absence of definitive judgment.

3

This exercise provides an opportunity for the reader to practice the skill of objective communication, developing greater awareness of their thoughts and words. Reflect on the power of non-judgment and begin to understand how the use of words can influence relationships and emotional well-being. Start telling your story...

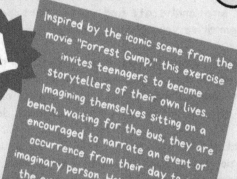

_____

_____

_____

_____

 BUS STOP

_____

_____

_____

Guiding to Success

Let's continue exploring the concept of being effective in your actions and achieving your goals. Understanding that success depends on our ability to <u>do what works</u> is essential. Focus on strategies and activities that bring you closer to the desired outcome.

Do not let emotions control your behaviour. Learn to <u>separate what you feel from what you do</u>. Emotions can often push you to make impulsive decisions or overreact. Take control and cut the string between your emotional state and your actions. You need to be able to recognize your emotions but do not let them drive your choices. Consciously choose how to act.

Another essential aspect is <u>respecting rules</u>. Rules may vary depending on the environment you are in, whether it's at home, school, or work. Respecting rules means understanding that they are essential for maintaining social order and promoting harmonious coexistence. Consider the consequences of your actions and make conscious decisions that respect the established rules.

Being practical also means acting skillfully to achieve your goals. Focus on what is necessary in the present situation instead of trying to fit your actions into ideal or more comfortable conditions. Do what is required in the context you are in. Adopt appropriate *strategies* to achieve the desired results. When necessary, dare to make tough choices and implement what works best for you.

Another crucial aspect is <u>letting go</u> of negative feelings and "should" that can hinder your path. Useless anger and the desire for revenge will not help you achieve your goals. Let these negative emotions dissolve, and instead, focus on constructive actions. Also, abandon the "should" that puts you under pressure with unrealistic expectations. Embrace reality and focus on what you can do to improve the situation.

Mindfulness is a valuable ally on the journey to effectiveness. It will help you observe and accept your thoughts, emotions, and actions without judgment. Develop an awareness of how your choices influence the results you obtain. Mindfulness will support you in building a solid foundation for a fulfilling and effectiveness-centred life.

Remember, you have the power to determine your effectiveness. Learn from your experiences and adopt the strategies that work best for you.

_____

_____

_____

_____

_____

_____

_____

_____

EXERCISE 15:
Choose Effectiveness

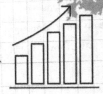

15 mins

Objective: develop awareness of what is "right" versus what is "effective" to make choices that lead to the desired outcome.

STEP 01

Imagine being involved in a situation where you need to make a decision. It could be a conflict with a friend, a school career choice, or a problem to solve at home. In this exercise, the goal is to reflect on what is "right" versus what is "effective" and make a choice based on effectiveness.

STEP 02

Take a moment to reflect on the specific situation you are facing. Identify different perspectives and possible solutions.

STEP 03

Ask yourself if what you consider "right" in the situation is truly the most effective choice. Consider if strong emotions or biases may influence your position. Carefully observe the consequences of the different available options. Consider which choice might lead to the best outcome for yourself and others involved.

STEP 04

After carefully considering the adequacy of different options, decide based on effectiveness. Choose what will lead you towards the desired outcome and promote a peaceful and positive resolution. Then observe how you feel about your decision and whether you have achieved the desired results.

05 STEP

What is "right" can be subjective and influenced by multiple factors. The goal of this exercise is to encourage you to consider effectiveness as the primary guide in your decision-making, allowing you to achieve positive and satisfying results.

Note:

It is important to emphasize that if the exercise involves complex or delicate situations, it is always advisable to seek the support of a trusted adult, such as a parent, teacher, or therapist, for further advice and assistance in making relevant decisions.

It to

EXERCISE 16:

Break Free from Chains

 Accept the presence of negative thoughts. They are your chains. Learn to let them go, fostering more significant mental serenity and effective decision-making.

Step 01

Imagine having a

conflict with very close friends. During an argument, your thoughts were "They insulted me" or "They think they can make fun of me" These negative thoughts have caused a strong sense of betrayal and anger within you As a result, you reacted impulsively by saying hurtful things or avoiding your friends.

Step 02

Describe the negative

thoughts you had in that situation For example, you may have thought, "I'm not a Winner," "No one understands me," or "I will never get over this hurdle."

Step 03

Reflect on how

those negative thoughts influenced your actions and your mood. Describe the steps you took and how you felt at that moment.

- Take a moment to observe that negative thoughts are just thoughts and not reality. Recognize that intense emotions can influence them and can lead to impulsive behaviour.

- Let go of the negative thoughts: imagine putting them in a cloud and letting them float away. Visualize this cloud slowly dissolving in the sky. Take deep breaths and relax, decreasing the tension and mental burden.

- Replace with positive thoughts: now, replace the negative thoughts with more positive and realistic reviews. For example, you could think, "I can learn from my mistakes and grow," "I have people who support me," or "I can face the challenges that come my way."

Step

04

After letting go

of the negative thoughts and replacing them with more positive reviews, reflect on the experience. Notice if your mood has improved and you have made more effective decisions without being controlled by negative emotions.

Letting go of

negative thoughts requires practice and patience. Remember that it is normal to have negative thoughts, but you can learn to manage them healthily. If you find it challenging to do it alone, don't hesitate to talk to a trusted adult, such as a parent, teacher, or therapist, who can offer you additional support and guidance.

Focus

Are you ready to explore the power of focus? In the hustle and bustle of everyday life, it's easy to get lost in distractions and scatter your energy. But learning to stay focused can make all the difference! Here are some tips to develop this skill:

- ☺ **The Magic of the Present Moment**: focus on the here and now. Let the past stay in the past, and the future wait its turn. Please direct your attention to the activities you're engaged in now, immersing yourself fully in them.

- ☺ **Forget about multitasking!** Concentrate on one thing at a time. Dedicate your time and energy to one task at a time, enjoying each step of the process. You'll see how much more productive and fulfilling it can be.

- ☺ **Distractions can be irresistible**, but you can learn to dance with them. Recognize them when they arise, acknowledge them, and then gently let them go. Keep your goal in sight and remain focused on what truly matters.

- ☺ **Some everyday actions** require little attention. Seize these opportunities to train your focus. For example, when brushing your teeth or taking a walk, be aware of each movement, each sensation, and each breath.

- ☺ **Focus is like a muscle**; it needs training. You can practice mindfulness exercises, such as focusing on your breath or visualization, to enhance your ability to stay present and focused.

Remember, focus helps you become more efficient, reach your goals, and fully appreciate your experiences. Take the time to develop this skill, and you'll discover the power within your focused mind.

Now, let's continue with the exercises to help you practice staying focused.

_____

_____

_____

_____

_____

_____

_____

_____

_____

_____

EXERCISE 17:
A Beautiful Mind Stay Present

In this exercise,

I will guide you through a specific activity to develop your ability to stay focused on the present. Choose one of the following activities and follow the instructions to put your concentration skills into practice.

1 Take a sheet of paper and

Take a sheet of paper and a pen or pencil. Choose an object or scene that you find exciting or meaningful. It could be a flower, a landscape, an object in your room, or anything that captures your attention. Place the object or picture in front of you or vividly imagine it.

4 Continue the drawing

With patience and care, dedicating time to each detail. Let the process itself become an experience of concentration and mental presence.

2 Carefully observe

the object or picture, paying attention to the details. Notice the shapes, colours, lines, and shadows that compose it. Start drawing the object or picture on paper, trying to reproduce what you see or imagine accurately.

ATTENTION

3 Focus on your hand

as it moves the pen or pencil on the paper. Feel the pressure, the fluidity of the movement, and the interaction between your hand and the sheet. Keep your attention focused on the drawing, letting other distractions fade away. If your mind wanders, gently bring your attention back to the picture.

5 Once you have

completed the drawing, please take a moment to observe it and reflect on how you feel after dedicating time to concentration and attention to detail.

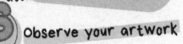

6 Observe your artwork

and take a moment to appreciate your effort and ability to concentrate. Practice this exercise regularly. O Choose different objects or repeat the same drawing to develop your ability to focus on the present and experience greater awareness of the details surrounding you.

_____

_____

_____

_____

_____

_____

EXERCISE 18:
Delicious Food

Get ready to
experience an engaging concentration exercise that involves preparing your favourite dish.

Objective: train concentration and attention through food preparation.

Choose your favourite
dish that you want to prepare. Make sure you have all the necessary ingredients within reach. Find a quiet and clean place in the kitchen to concentrate without distractions.

01

Put away your phone and
other devices that could interrupt your focus. This is your time to fully dedicate yourself to preparing the dish. Start arranging the ingredients on the table, carefully observing each one. Notice the colours and their aromas.

02

Focus on the actions
you are taking as you prepare the dish. Cut the ingredients carefully and mix them in the right amounts, following the recipe attentively. Feel the movement of your hands as you work with the ingredients. Observe the texture of the food taking shape.

03

Slow down the pace and
tune in to the details of the cooking process. Notice how the ingredients transform as they combine to create a delightful result. During the process, try to notice your thoughts and emotions that arise. Accept them without judgment but remain focused on the task at hand.

04

Maintain a mindful connection with your senses:

- Taste the ingredients.
- Feel their aromas spreading in the room.
- Observe the dish's change in colour and texture.

05

During the meal, focus on

the food's flavours, textures, and sensory experience. Let each bite be an opportunity to immerse yourself in the present moment fully.

06

07

Once the dish is ready

serve it with care and take a moment to appreciate the outcome of your work. Sit down, take deep breaths, and savour each bite with mindfulness and gratitude.

After finishing the meal, reflect on your experience. Notice if you have experienced increased <u>awareness</u>, <u>concentration</u>, and <u>enjoyment</u> while preparing and consuming the food.

Chapter 3: Emotions

EMOTION REGULATION

In the first subchapter of this chapter, we will explore **strategies** for emotional regulation in DBT. Emotion regulation is a powerful skill that helps us manage the emotions we want to change or reduce in intensity. It makes us less vulnerable to extreme emotions and increases our emotional resilience. Emotional regulation requires mindfulness, particularly observing and non-judgmentally describing our current emotions.

Emotions are complex phenomena and consist of parts that occur simultaneously. We can influence the entire emotion by changing one aspect of this emotional response. Understanding the different components of emotions can help us modify them more effectively.

Awareness of current emotions involves observing, describing, and accepting our feelings without judgment or attempting to change, block, or distract ourselves from them. Avoiding or suppressing emotions only increases our suffering. Awareness of current emotions is the path to emotional freedom and is a fundamental skill in DBT.

When emotions are highly intense, our regulation skills may be disrupted. It is essential to recognize when we reach the breaking point of our skills, which indicates the need to use crisis survival skills.

Letting go of emotional suffering is an essential first step. Observe your emotions without judgment and take note of the physical sensations you feel in your body. Remember that you are not your emotions but can learn to love and respect them. Practice radically accepting your emotions, allowing them to exist without trying to change them.

When emotions are overwhelming and exceed our capacity for regulation, we can employ specific strategies. Begin by observing and describing the point at which you reach the limit of your abilities:

- ☠ Your distress is extreme.
- ☠ You feel overwhelmed.
- ☠ Your mind is solely focused on the emotion itself.
- ☠ Your mind seems to "shut down," and rational thinking becomes difficult.
- ☠ You need help with problem-solving or using complex skills.

If you find yourself in this state of distress, you have reached the breaking point of your abilities. It is time to use crisis survival skills to reduce emotional arousal:

- ☻ For example, your body's chemistry can be affected by immersing your face in cold water or drinking something cold.
- ☻ **Distract** from the emotional events by focusing on something different or engaging in a pleasurable activity.
- ☻ **Self-Soothe** means relaxing through your five senses, using pleasant impulses such as listening to relaxing music, touching a soft texture, or savouring a food you enjoy.
- ☻ **Improve** the moment by fully paying attention to the here and now and experiencing the present moment.

These strategies can help you manage extreme emotions and restore a sense of calm and control.

_____
_____
_____
_____
_____
_____
_____
_____
_____
_____
_____
_____
_____
_____
_____
_____

EXERCISE 19:

Extreme

It is important to develop awareness of your emotions and learn to regulate them effectively. Take some time to engage in this exercise of observing and regulating emotions. Find a quiet and comfortable place to dedicate yourself to this practice entirely.

1 Sit comfortably, close your eyes, and begin to focus on your breath. Breathe deeply, feeling the air entering and leaving your body. Relax your muscles and try to release any accumulated tension.

your eyes closed, bring your attention to your emotions. Notice which emotions are emerging. They may be joy, sadness, anger, fear, or other emotions. Observe them without judgment, simply becoming aware of their presence.

2 Observe your emotions: With

3 With your eyes still closed

start describing your emotions out loud or in your mind. Use words that define them, such as "joy," "sadness," "anger," or "fear." Try to be as detailed as possible in describing each emotion.

your emotions, please choose one of them to work on. Focus on that specific emotion and experience how it manifests in your body. Notice if there are any tensions or physical sensations associated with it.

4 After observing and describing

5 Imagine taking a deep breath and

slowly releasing that specific emotion as you exhale. Imagine the feeling dissolving and moving away from you, making space for calm and tranquillity. Repeat this process for a few minutes, entirely focusing on regulating that specific emotion.

during this process of emotional regulation. If the emotion returns or other emotions emerge, repeat the process of observation and regulation.

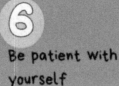 

6 Be patient with yourself

more emotions, slowly open your eyes and take a moment to observe how you feel. Notice if there is any change in the intensity or quality of the feelings you explored. Reflect on your experience and awareness of your emotions. Consider how you can apply this practice of observing and regulating emotions in your everyday life when faced with emotionally intense situations.

7 Conclusion: After working on one or

Remember that emotional

regulation is a skill that requires practice and patience. Repeat this exercise whenever you wish to explore and manage your emotions more mindfully and effectively.

_____

_____

_____

_____

_____

_____

_____

_____

_____

_____

_____

ACTING IN THE OPPOSITE WAY

Emotions can be complex and sometimes do not correspond to reality. When acting based on emotions is ineffective, we can adopt an opposite approach to change our emotional reactions. Here are some concepts to keep in mind:

+ **Examine your thoughts**: often, our emotions result from our thoughts and interpretations of events. Our emotions can significantly influence how we perceive these events. Take the time to reflect on your thoughts and verify the objective facts. It will help you change your emotions.

+ **Know your emotions**: it is essential to identify and understand the feelings you feel. Observe and describe your emotions, giving them a name. Also, consider how your emotions may impact your current well-being. This awareness allows you to take control of your emotions more effectively.

+ **Reduce emotional vulnerability**: the goal is to reduce exposure to unwanted emotions and increase positive ones. You can do this by following strategies that help you manage your emotions healthy and balanced. The practice of mindfulness and awareness plays a crucial role in this process.

+ **Change emotions through contrary action**: when you find yourself in a harmful or inappropriate emotional state, you can try to change your emotions by acting oppositely. This means behaving in a way that contrasts with the emotion you are experiencing. For example, try doing something joyful or fun if you feel sad. If you feel angry, find a way to calm down and relax.

+ **Check the facts**: emotions are not necessarily based on facts. Often, our emotions indicate what is happening, but it is essential to verify the facts of that situation. Your emotions are not an absolute truth, so strive to have an objective view.

+ **Emotions influence others**: Our emotions concern us and can influence those around us. Our facial expressions, tone of voice, and body posture can communicate to others what we are experiencing emotionally. Be aware of how your emotions influence interactions with others and how that can impact your relationship.

+ **Emotions as a driving force for action**: Emotions motivate and prepare us for action. They are a signal from our body to act in certain situations. Strong emotions help us overcome obstacles and react quickly and appropriately. However, it is important to learn how to manage emotions healthily and channel them into constructive actions.

Take this information and reflect on how you can apply it daily. The goal is to develop emotional awareness and manage your emotions effectively to promote your well-being and relationships with others.

_____

_____

_____

EXERCISE 20:
Swimming Upstream

Experience the power of acting opposite to your emotions to change your mood and achieve positive outcomes.

This exercise invites you to

put into practice the experience of acting opposite to your emotions. Follow the steps below to reverse your emotional state:

Imagine feeling nervous about

an upcoming school exam. Your emotions make you feel insecure and discouraged about your chances of success.

⊛ Become aware of your emotions in the present moment. Recognize the nervousness, insecurity, and discouragement you are experiencing.

✳ The opposite action to these emotions could be visualizing yourself calmly and confidently taking the exam. Imagine the success and satisfaction you feel after passing the exam with positive results.

✳ Imagine sitting in a quiet place and closing your eyes. Take deep breaths and visualize yourself calmly and confidently facing the exam. Imagine answering the questions accurately and feeling pride and satisfaction at the end of the exam.

✳ After performing the opposite action, observe how you feel. Notice if your emotional state has changed, and if you feel more confident, motivated, or capable of approaching the exam with a positive mindset. Take note of any changes in your attitude or perspective.

✳ At the end of the exercise, reflect on how acting opposite to your emotions has influenced your mood and approach to the stressful situation. Take note of any learning or realization you gained during the exercise.

Repeat this exercise whenever you

want to reverse your negative emotions or when your feelings are not leading you to positive outcomes. Remember that acting the opposite can help strengthen your confidence and manage stress more effectively, enabling you to face challenges with a more positive perspective.

ABC

Accumulate Experiences - Short-term: Fill Yourself With Joy

Take time for activities that bring you happiness and positive emotions. Choose things that you genuinely enjoy and that make you feel good. Remember the positive episodes you have experienced, those special moments that made you smile. When you have a positive experience, fully focus on it, immersing yourself completely in the present moment. Avoid letting worries or negative thoughts steal the joy of the moment from you.

Accumulate Experiences - Long-term: Build a Life Worth Living

Don't settle for just small moments of happiness; strive to create a life filled with positive experiences. Think about what truly makes you happy and fulfilled. Identify goals that align with your values and plan the necessary steps to achieve them. It may seem challenging initially, but every small step will bring you closer to realizing your dreams. Don't give up; persist in pursuing what truly brings you happiness.

Emotions are a part of you, but they <u>do not define who you are</u>. You are aware of your emotions, so allow them to flow and manifest, but do not let them dominate you. Focus on the <u>positive aspects</u> of situations, <u>letting go</u> of worries and excessive expectations. Live each moment with gratitude and openness, allowing positive experiences to enrich your life.

_____
_____
_____
_____
_____
_____
_____
_____
_____
_____
_____
_____
_____
_____
_____

EXERCISE 21:
Scrapbook

Objective: Accumulate and preserve positive experiences to nurture happiness and gratitude in your life.

1 Take the time to create a

"Happiness Scrapbook," an album that gathers special moments and positive memories. This exercise will help you grow a positive perspective, focus on joyful experiences, and develop a sense of gratitude for what you have lived.

2 Gather the necessary

materials for your scrapbook: an empty album or notebook, scissors, glue, colour pens, stickers, and any other decorations you like.

3 Take the time to create a

Dedicate time to reflect on the positive experiences you have had recently. These could be moments of joy, personal successes, kind gestures from others, or anything that has made you happy. Make a list of these experiences to remember while creating your scrapbook.

4 Choose the pages where

you want to place your positive experiences. Cut out photos, images, or newspaper clippings representing these special moments. Add descriptions or notes to remember the details and emotions associated with each experience. Be creative in arranging the elements and decorating the pages.

5 As you work on your scrapbook

take the time to reflect on the positive experiences you are documenting. Observe how they make you feel and how they have influenced your mood. Express gratitude for these experiences and for the people who made them possible. Write a few words of thanks or appreciation next to each page.

6 Once you have completed your

scrapbook, take the time to review it and read your reflections. Show it to trusted individuals, such as friends or family, and share your positive experiences. Consider sharing the pages of your scrapbook on social media, only if you feel comfortable doing so, to inspire and spread some happiness among others.

Benefits:

- Increase awareness of positive experiences in your life.
- Cultivate an optimistic and grateful perspective.
- Create an album of positive memories to revisit when you need a dose of happiness.
- Strengthen appreciation for the people and circumstances that bring joy to your life.

Remember that this is

an ongoing project, so continue adding new positive experiences and decorating the pages as you live unique moments.

Enjoy creating your scrapbook, and may it bring you much joy and gratitude!

_____
_____
_____
_____
_____
_____
_____
_____
_____

After this exciting exercise, let's move forward with our discussion. You should know that our relationships with others are fundamental in our lives. They can bring joy, support, connection, stress, and pain. In your personal growth, paying attention to relationships, working on existing ones and creating new ones while avoiding toxic links is essential.

Sometimes, relationships can be damaged or challenged by conflicts or misunderstandings. This exercise invites you to consider which relationships might need care and how you could work to repair them. It might involve having an open and honest conversation, offering apologies, forgiving, or seeking compromise. Remember that relationships require commitment and effort from both sides.

New relationships can enrich our lives and offer opportunities for growth and connection. Explore new environments, participate in events or activities that interest you, and be open to meeting new people. Practice empathy, kindness, and availability in building meaningful bonds with others.

Existing relationships can benefit from ongoing attention and care. Dedicate quality time to the important people in your life. Listen attentively, express appreciation, share your emotions, and offer support when needed. Strive to create an environment of trust and mutual understanding.

Sometimes, certain relationships can become toxic or harmful to our well-being. If you find yourself in a relationship that consistently brings you stress, pain, or unhappiness, it is important to consider the possibility of ending it. This may require courage and support from friends, family, or professionals. Remember that your happiness and well-being are essential.

Avoiding confronting issues or delaying important decisions can increase your emotional vulnerability:
1. Face challenges and difficulties with courage and determination.
2. Do not postpone necessary conversations or actions that can lead to a positive resolution.
3. Remember that taking control of situations can lead to more excellent emotional stability.

Don't give up. In life, there will always be difficult moments and complex situations. However, it is important not to give up in adversity. Challenge yourself to overcome obstacles by seeking creative solutions and learning from mistakes. Maintain a positive mindset and trust in yourself.
Take care of your relationships and know how they can influence your emotional well-being. You can create meaningful connections and maintain healthy and satisfying relationships with suitable attention and commitment.

Engaging in activities that challenge your skills is crucial to feeling competent and in control of your life. Choose at least one thing each day that allows you to grow and improve. It could be assembling furniture, learning to play an instrument, or starting a new project. The goal is to tackle something difficult but possible and gradually increase the challenge over time. If a challenge seems too tricky initially, start with something more accessible and progress step by step.

If you want to deal with situations that may generate negative emotions effectively, it is helpful to prepare in advance. Please describe the problem in detail, paying attention to the facts and separating them from your interpretations. Identify the emotions you might experience in that situation. Vividly imagine the case in your mind, fully immersing yourself in it. Mentally rehearse how you will effectively handle the situation, envisioning the actions, thoughts, and words you will use. Practice problem-solving for any issues, stimulating your creativity and exploring different possible solutions. Please choose the answer you deem most suitable and put it into practice. Evaluate the results obtained and make any necessary adjustments.

_____

_____

_____

_____

Looking to the Future: It means having a positive outlook and focusing on the goals you want to achieve. Identify goals based on your values. Make a list of small steps to get closer to these goals. You can start by brainstorming many possible solutions, choosing the most suitable one, and then implementing it. Monitor the results and evaluate if you are making progress.

Mastering fear and looking to the future requires commitment and consistent practice. Experiment with these strategies and discover how they can help you develop self-confidence and overcome life's challenges. Remember that you can master your fears and build a better future.

Chapter 4: Facing the Storm

DISTRESS TOLERANCE

The ability to tolerate troubles is fundamental for handling crises without making things worse and for accepting reality to move forward.

Distress Tolerance is the ability to endure and survive crises without further escalation. This skill allows us to accept reality, replacing suffering and feeling "stuck" with ordinary pain and the possibility of moving on. Additionally, it frees us from the need to immediately satisfy our most intense desires, urges, and emotions.

Tolerance for discomfort is essential for two reasons. 1. pain and distress are integral to life and cannot be avoided entirely or eliminated. The inability to accept this inevitable reality can amplify the pain and suffering we experience. 2. tolerance for discomfort is necessary for any short-term personal change process. If we cannot tolerate temporary distress and pain, our efforts to avoid or escape such experiences will interfere with achieving the desired changes.

In the context of DBT, various techniques are available to develop distress tolerance. These include relaxation techniques, visualization, and distraction, which can be employed to cope with stress and adverse situations.

Moreover, it is essential to reduce impulsive behaviours, often resulting from acting without reflection, fleeing, or avoiding emotional experiences. Tolerance for discomfort can help reduce impulsivity, enabling more constructive engagement with difficult situations.

The goal is to increase the capacity to tolerate discomfort. This involves learning to manage pain and distress without resorting to destructive behaviours. Developing distress tolerance allows for more effective coping with life's challenges and maintaining mental and emotional well-being.

Crisis Toolkit

In DBT, crisis survival skills are essential for overcoming crises without further exacerbating them. It is important to remember that troubles are, by definition, short-term. Crisis survival skills aim to provide practical strategies for dealing with these difficult situations.

The appropriate time to use these skills is when facing a highly stressful situation, having a short duration, and requiring an immediate solution. These skills are handy when the pain is intense and cannot be quickly alleviated, when there is a desire to regulate emotions without worsening the situation and when the emotional mind threatens to overwhelm us. We need a bright mind, and when we are overwhelmed but demands must be met or excitement is extreme, we cannot resolve problems immediately.

It is important to note that we should refrain from using crisis survival skills to solve everyday problems or attempt to address all of life's challenges. Their primary function is to provide practical tools for specific crises. However, these skills can play a significant role in providing emotional stability during difficult times.

It is crucial to understand that crisis survival skills are not a substitute for addressing underlying issues more thoroughly. They are temporary tools that can help manage the present moment and prevent the situation from worsening. To resolve problems more comprehensively, further exploration of other skills and specific strategies may be necessary.

Finally, a crisis toolkit alone cannot make one's life worth living. These skills provide vital support during times of difficulty. Still, working on other areas of life, such as emotional well-being and interpersonal relationships, and discovering personal meaning and purpose is essential.

Emotional Balance

Emotion regulation skills are crucial in DBT to help teenagers manage their emotions healthily and constructively. Among these skills, the STOP Skills are practical tools for interrupting automatic reactive patterns and taking control of one's emotional response.

The **STOP Skills** involve four key steps:

- S - **Stop**: In these moments of intense emotional involvement, stopping, pausing, and refraining from acting hastily is essential to halting impulsive reactions. The goal is to maintain control over actions rather than being driven by emotions.

- T - **Step Back**: Take a deep breath and mentally distance yourself from the situation. This will create space between you and your emotions, enabling you to observe them more objectively.

- O - **Observe**: once you have stopped and created distance, note what is happening within and around you. Notice your thoughts and feelings and what others are saying or doing. This awareness helps you better understand the situation and recognize your emotional reactions.

- P - **Proceed Mindfully**: When it comes time to decide how to act, do so with mindfulness. Consider your thoughts and feelings, the situation, and the perspectives of others. Reflect on your goals and ask yourself (use Wise Mind) which actions will improve or worsen the case in the long run.

The STOP Skills offer a practical approach to regulating emotions in critical moments. Teenagers can develop greater emotional mastery and make more mindful decisions through awareness and control of their reactions.

Decision Making

Decision-making skills are crucial for adolescents who strive to make conscious choices that promote their long-term well-being. Using "Pros and Cons" is a helpful tool for assessing different options and weighing their positive and negative effects.

Here's how to utilize this strategy:

- ☒ We are **identifying crises**. Recognize when an impulse transforms into concern when it becomes highly intense, and acting upon it would worsen the situation in the long run.

- ☒ Listing the **pros and cons of acting** on the impulse. Make a list of the advantages and disadvantages of following the crisis impulse. These may include dangerous, addictive, or harmful behaviours and sacrificing or avoiding building the life you desire.

- ☒ Listing the **pros and cons of resisting** the impulses. Create another list of the benefits and drawbacks of opposing crisis impulses, tolerating distress, and not giving in to impulsive behaviours.

- ☒ **Write down** your pros and cons list and carry them with you. Repeat the positive and negative points multiple times to reinforce your awareness.

- ☒ When the overwhelming impulse strikes, **review** your pros and cons lists. Focus on the positive consequences of resisting the impulse and reflect on the negative impacts of succumbing to crisis behaviours. Consider past experiences, such as acting on impulses, which led to undesirable outcomes.

_____

_____

_____

_____

_____

_____

_____

_____

_____

EXERCISE 22:
Trick or Treat?

10 mins

Think about an event of the past that evoked intense emotions, one in which you still remember your state of mind and behaviours. Mentally reprocess that situation and reflect on the positive consequences that would have occurred if you had resisted that emotion. Then, recall the negative consequences you experienced by giving in to that crisis.

1 Take a sheet of paper and draw a cross. In the top-left quadrant, write down the favourable aspects of "acting" on the impulses, while in the top-right quadrant, write down the negative aspects.

2 In the bottom-left quadrant note the positive aspects of "resisting" the impulses and doing what was necessary without giving in. In the right part of this quadrant, write down the negative aspects.

3 You will notice that when your mind is clear, free from the stress of emotions, it can describe what happened analytically. Remember to avoid judgments and focus solely on the facts.

4 This exercise will be valuable to you when you feel your emotions are taking control of your mind. Use it to regain mental clarity and make decisions based on awareness.

OPEN MIND

WOW!

Regulate Pressure

TIPP skills are quick and effective for reducing high emotional arousal when facing intense emotions:

- ⊙ T - **Temperature** (cold water),
- ⊙ I - **Intense Exercise,**
- ⊙ P - **Paced Breathing** and
- ⊙ P - **Paired Muscle Relaxation.**

Cooling the face with cold water: This technique allows for quick calming. Cold water triggers an immediate drop-in heart rate. However, it's essential to consult with your doctor before using this technique.

Intense physical exercise to calm the body: engaging in intense physical activity, even briefly, can help dissipate excessive emotional energy stored in the body. Running, brisk walking, jumping, playing basketball, or weightlifting are just a few exercises you can do. Again, it is essential to consult with your doctor before.

_____

_____

_____

_____

_____

_____

_____

_____

_____

_____

_____

_____

_____

_____

_____

_____

_____

_____

EXERCISE 23:
Relax

10 mins

Ensure you are relaxed, releasing any muscle tension and allowing your body's weight to sink into the supporting surface.

1 Close your eyes and begin to focus on your breath. Slowly inhale, counting to four. Then exhale gently, counting to six. Try to breathe deeply and evenly, releasing any tension as you exhale. Now, imagine yourself in a beautiful garden surrounded by nature. Picture the sun gently warming your skin and the soothing sound of water flowing from a nearby fountain.

2 Start to explore the garden in your mind. Walk along a welcoming path and observe the colourful flowers blooming. Notice the vibrant colours and delicate scents filling the air. Not far away, there is a bench under a shady tree. Sit on the bench and feel your body completely relaxing. You can feel the gentle breeze caressing your face and the sense of peace enveloping you.

3 Now, shift your attention to each part of your body. Imagine a warm and relaxing light gently resting upon you, starting from the top of your head and slowly descending to your neck, shoulders, chest, arms, hands, legs, and feet. Feel how this light melts away any tension and gives you a pleasant sensation of lightness and peace.

4 Stay seated or on the bench momentarily, enjoying the calm and relaxation surrounding you. Feel how your entire body is relaxed and at ease. When ready, gradually open your eyes and return to present awareness. Carry this sense of calm and relaxation with you throughout your day, knowing you can return to this place of inner peace whenever needed.

This guided journey to calmness offers a moment of pause and relaxation, temporarily allowing you to escape from everyday stress and worries. Use it to find serenity and strengthen your mind and body.

Energy for Mind and Body

Breathing is a fundamental process, yet we are only sometimes aware of its transformative potential. Accelerated breathing is a technique that allows us to connect with our body, increase energy levels, and reduce stress.

We often breathe shallowly and rapidly under pressure or in intense situations. This limited type of breathing can heighten anxiety and tension in our bodies. Accelerated breathing, on the other hand, offers us the opportunity to reverse this tendency and experience a new form of vitality.

Accelerated breathing is a technique that involves pacing our breath, intentionally speeding it up in a controlled manner. Breathing this way sends a message to our nervous system that stimulates energy production and activates our mind.

This technique can be helpful in various situations, such as when we need an energy boost before an important event, when we feel exhausted, or when we want to enhance our focus and concentration.

During the practice of accelerated breathing, you may notice an increase in your heart rate and a sensation of vitality spreading throughout your body. This signifies that your system responds to the technique and receives a refreshing energy flow. You may experience a sense of renewed mental and physical energy, greater mental clarity, and increased concentration.

Remember that accelerated breathing can be practised at different times of the day, depending on your needs. Listening to your body and practising this technique safely and mindfully is essential.

So, the next time you desire an effective way to energize your mind and body, try accelerated breathing and enjoy its benefits in your daily life. Experience the sensation of vitality and power that this practice can offer you, and let your breath become a source of positive energy.

_____

_____

_____

_____

_____

_____

_____

_____

_____

_____

_____

EXERCISE 24:
Deep Breath Flow

10 mins

Find a quiet and comfortable place to sit or lie down. Ensure that you are in a relaxed position with a straight back and open shoulders.

1 **Close your eyes and** begin to focus on your breath. Bring awareness to your breath as it flows in and out of your body.

2 **Imagine your breath as** a gentle stream of water flowing in a river. Imagine dipping your fingers into the cool water and feeling its softness and freshness as it flows between them.

3 **Start to breathe** slowly, bringing the air into your belly. Count to four during the inspiration, feeling your abdomen expand as it fills with air.

4 **When you reach the peak of** the inspiration, begin to exhale slowly. Count to six during the breathing out, letting the air go in a controlled and relaxed manner. Imagine your breath as a flowing stream of water, carrying away tensions and stress.

5 **Continue to breathe this** way, focusing on the sensation of your breath and the slow steady rhythm. Each inhalation fills you with calmness and relaxation, while each exhalation releases tensions and worries.

6 **Stay in this practice of** deep breathing for a few minutes, allowing your breath to become slower and more peaceful. Feel how your mind calms down, and your body relaxes deeply.

7 **When ready, gradually open** your eyes and carry this inner peace throughout your day. Remember that you can always return to this practice of deep breathing whenever you desire to regain calmness and well-being.

8 **This exercise offers a** simple and effective way to slow down the pace of your breath and connect with your body and mind. Use it to alleviate stress and cultivate a sense of inner peace whenever you need it.

Restore Inner Peace

Muscle tension is a common symptom of daily stress and anxiety. **Empowered muscle relaxation** is a simple yet powerful technique that helps us release accumulated body tension, promoting a sense of calmness and tranquillity.

When we're under stress, our muscles contract and tighten, maintaining a constant tension that can negatively impact our physical and mental well-being. Empowered muscle relaxation offers an effective way to reverse this process and facilitate deep relaxation.

This technique involves combining muscle relaxation with the exhalation of the breath. During the exhalation, we focus on consciously relaxing our muscles, allowing them to loosen and release the accumulated tension.

After completing empowered muscle relaxation, take a moment to notice how you feel. As the tension gradually dissolves, you may experience a sense of lightness and serenity in your body.

Remember that this muscle relaxation can be practised at any time of the day, whenever you wish, to free yourself from stress and regain a sense of inner calm. It's a simple yet effective technique to integrate into your daily routine to promote well-being and stress management.

EXERCISE 25:

No More Stress

Sit or lie down in a comfortable position. Close your eyes and take a few deep breaths to catch your attention.

1

Begin to exhale slowly
imagining tensing the muscles in your face as you mentally say, "Relax." Release the tension as you inhale.

2
Continue to breathe relaxed, shifting your attention to your shoulders. During the exhalation, gently tense the muscles in your shoulders and release the tension as you inhale, repeating the word "Relax" in your mind.

3
Proceed with the process, shifting your focus to your arms, chest, stomach, legs, and feet. Concentrate on each part of your body, tensing the muscles during the exhalation and releasing the tension as you inhale.

4
Continue this exercise for a few minutes, allowing your body to relax and feel the calmness spreading. .

5
When you feel ready, gently open your eyes and take a moment to notice the effects of this simple paired muscle relaxation exercise on your body and mind. Resurface with a sense of calm, ready to face the rest of your day with serenity

Empowered muscle relaxation is a valuable resource you can use anytime to release accumulated tension and rediscover inner Well-being.

EXPLORE CREATIVITY

Distractions can become a valuable ally when faced with anxiety and difficult moments. They serve as a helpful tool to temporarily distance ourselves from what causes us distress or suffering, allowing us to recharge and find a bit of serenity. There are multiple ways to find beneficial distractions, and we invite you to explore them with curiosity and awareness.

Here are some suggestions for distractions that can help you regain balance and calm:

- ✪ Immerse yourself in **creative activities** that stimulate your imagination and allow you to express yourself differently. You could draw, paint, write poetry or stories, play a musical instrument, or create objects with your hands. Creativity can become a channel to <u>release emotions</u> and find a moment of inner peace.

- ✪ Seek support from others through **social connection**. You can call a friend, organize a video call with a loved one, participate in an online group activity, or join a forum or community where you can share common interests. Sharing experiences and feeling understood can <u>alleviate tensions</u> and give you a sense of belonging.

- ✪ Take advantage of nature's beauty and the beneficial effect of **movement**. Take a walk outdoors, cycle, or jog, or engage in a physical activity you enjoy. Fresh air, sunlight, and exercise can promote <u>mental relaxation</u> and provide you with an exhilarating break.

- ✪ Dedicate time to **fun** and activities that you genuinely enjoy. Watch a TV series or a movie that captivates you, listen to your favourite music, read an engaging book, or try new games or sports that intrigue you. Allow yourself to <u>break away from routine</u> and enjoy moments of pure pleasure.

- ✪ Explore meditation and mindfulness techniques to regain **balance**. You can practice mindful breathing, guided visualization, or engage in a meditation session. These practices will help you <u>focus on the present moment</u>, let go of negative thoughts, and cultivate inner calm.

- ✪ Dedicate precious time to **taking care of yourself**. You can take a long hot shower, have a relaxing bath, practice skincare, or prepare a soothing herbal tea. Discover what makes you <u>feel good</u> and pamper your body and mind.

- ✪ Challenge your mind with stimulating **intellectual activities**. Read interesting books, solve puzzles or crosswords, learn a new language, or learn more about a discipline that fascinates you. Nourishing your mind with knowledge and <u>curiosity</u> will help shift your attention away from distress.

Now is the time to explore these distractions wisely and find the ones that resonate most with you.

Remember that each person is unique, so choose distractions that best fit your personality and preferences. The goal is to find refuge in serenity, reactivate your vital energy, and maintain a positive mental state.

EXERCISE 26:
Creating Emotions

15 mins

This engaging exercise will guide you through an emotional journey filled with fun and distraction. As you discover how distractions can positively impact your emotional well-being, get ready to explore new activities and sensations. Imagine embarking on a unique emotional journey. Focus on your current emotions. What emotions are you experiencing right now? Note down these emotions.

Prepare a virtual map of

distractions by listing different activities that can divert your mind from negative emotions. Here are some suggestions:

1

A Take paper and coloured pencils and let your creativity flow.

Draw what inspires you or create artwork that represents your positive emotions.

B Create a playlist of songs that make you feel happy and energized.

Listen to it when you need an extra boost to face the day's challenges.

C Play your favourite song and dance as if nobody is watching.

Let the rhythm captivate you and release all the negative energy through the movements of your body.

D Organize a game with your friends, both online and in person.

Choose a game that brings you joy and spend carefree time with people who make you laugh.

E Dedicate time to mental and physical well-being through yoga or meditation.

Focus on your breath and let your mind calm down and relax.

F Experiment in the kitchen and try preparing a new recipe that fascinates you.

Get involved in the aromas and flavours and enjoy the pleasure of creating something delicious.

2 ### This map will guide you when you want
to distract your mind from worries and immerse yourself in positive and fulfilling activities. Remember to experiment and personalize the activities according to your tastes and interests.

Now that you have your distraction map choose

an emotional path to follow. Select a negative emotion you want to overcome or transform into a positive sensation. For example, you may wish to combat sadness and turn it into happiness or overcome anxiety to reach a sense of calm. Follow your instinct and choose the emotion that you feel inclined to tackle.

On your distraction map, identify three

activities corresponding to your chosen negative emotion. For instance, if you overcome sadness, you might listen to a playlist of cheerful songs, play with friends, or prepare a recipe.

Now it's time to begin your emotional journey

through distractions! Please choose one of the three activities you identified and fully immerse yourself in it. Focus on your actions, experience the sensations it evokes, and let your mind stray away from negative emotions. Enjoy every moment and note how your negative emotion gradually transforms or eases.

After completing each emotional activity, take a

moment to reflect on how you feel now compared to the beginning. Have your emotions changed? If so, in what way? Note these observations on your distraction map.

Repeat the process with the other two emotional

activities you selected. Explore the different distractions and observe how each one influences your emotional state. Experiment, have fun, and let these distractions guide your journey towards more positive emotions.

Final Reflection: What have you learned about

yourself and how distractions can influence your emotions? How can you apply this knowledge daily to manage your feelings better?

Remember that you can return to

this distraction map whenever you want to explore new activities to divert your mind from negative emotions and promote your emotional well-being.

SELF-SOOTHING

Self-soothing, or self-relaxation, is a way to <u>take care of yourself</u> by offering pleasure and comfort to reduce stress and pain. In this section, we will explore five ways to engage our senses to achieve a sense of calm and tranquillity.

Imagine exploring the "**Five Senses**" to discover how to self-relax:

- ⚫ **Vision**: find a quiet place and immerse yourself in a relaxing visual experience. Watch a colourful sunset, browse a photography book, or create a collage of your favourite images. Take time to observe nature or create artwork expressing your unique world vision.

- ⚫ **Hearing**: focus on sounds that relax and put you at ease. Listen to your favourite music, carried away by melodies or meaningful song lyrics. Spend time enjoying the sounds of nature, such as the rustling of leaves or the singing of birds. Create your playlist of relaxing tunes or explore new music genres that appeal to you.

- ⚫ **Smell**: explore a scent that makes you feel good and provides calm. Light a scented candle or diffuse essential oils with relaxing fragrances like lavender or vanilla. Prepare a cup of aromatic tea or coffee and enjoy the scent that fills the air. Take a walk outdoors and let the scents of nature envelop you.

- ⚫ **Taste**: dedicate time to experiencing flavours that bring you pleasure and relaxation. Prepare a cup of hot chocolate, savouring each sip slowly. Taste the sweet flavour of fresh fruit or your favourite dessert. Explore new tastes and cook a dish that you particularly enjoy. Experiment with unique flavours and delight in the sensations that taste can offer.

- ⚫ **Touch**: focus on tactile sensations that bring you comfort and well-being. Take a shower or a warm bath, letting the water caress your skin. Wrap yourself in a soft blanket or wear clothing that gives you a sense of calmness. Take time to gently massage your hands or feet, enjoying the soothing contact. Explore different materials like sand, wood, or fabrics to discover new tactile sensations.

Experiment with the "Five Senses" to create a unique self-relaxation experience. Depending on your preferences and the situations you find yourself in, you can combine multiple senses or focus on a specific one.

Remember that self-relaxation is a way to care for yourself and <u>cultivate lasting emotional well-being</u>. Explore, discover, and give yourself time to self-relax through your senses, filling your life with pleasure and peace.

_____

_____

_____

_____

_____

EXERCISE 27:

Sensory Jogging

Get ready for an exciting

sensory adventure during your movement session! Follow these steps for an engaging and original experience:

Choose an unconventional route for your physical activity, such as a park with a winding trail or a natural area with different terrains. Look for an environment that offers a variety of sensory stimuli. **A**

During your run, take the time to observe your surroundings closely. Admire the beauty of nature, the details of flowers and trees, vibrant colours, or delicate shades. Please pay attention to the small wonders that often escape our notice. **B**

Focus on the sounds around you. Listen to the birds singing, the rustling of leaves, the wind whispering through the trees. Let the sounds envelop you and connect you with the natural environment. **C**

Take a short break during your route to enjoy a small energy snack. Choose foods different from your usual choices, such as exotic fruit or a healthy snack with unusual flavours. Focus on the tastes and enjoy the moment of pleasure. **D**

Seek direct contact with nature during your run. You can touch the grass, the leaves of trees, or the water from a stream. Experience the different textures and temperatures you encounter along the way. **E**

During the run, bring your attention to your breath. Breathe deeply and consciously, focusing on the air entering and leaving your body. Feel how your breath aligns with the energy and rhythm of the surrounding nature. **F**

Jogging

As you immerse yourself in your sensory adventure, take moments to express gratitude for the beauty and harmony of nature. Be aware of the privileges you have in being able to experience this combination of movement and sensations.

Remember

this sensory adventure aims to stimulate all your senses and create a deep connection with the environment around you. Be open to the surprise wilderness offers and let yourself be carried away by the sensations that arise during the journey.

ENHANCING CRISIS SCENARIOS

You can use numerous strategies to enhance the quality of the present moment and navigate a crisis without worsening it.

IMPROVE is a simple way to remember these strategies that can assist you. Let's explore what it means:

→ **I - Imagery**: Visualizes vivid and relaxing scenes of a peaceful and safe place. Mentally picture things resolving positively and imagine yourself successfully facing and overcoming them. See negative emotions flowing away like water from a pipe.

→ **M - Meaning**:
1. Find or create purpose, meaning, or value in the pain you are experiencing.
2. Seek to transform difficulties into opportunities for personal growth.
3. Find meaning even in the small things and strive to find a positive point of view in challenging situations.

→ **P - Prayer**: Open yourself to the higher power you believe in or the inner wisdom that guides you. Turn to a force greater than yourself, seeking the strength and courage to face and overcome the crisis.

→ **R - Relaxing Actions**:
1. Dedicate time to relaxing your body and mind.
2. Practice relaxation techniques such as deep breathing, stretching, listening to soothing music, or meditation.
3. Treat yourself to a warm bath or massage to alleviate accumulated tension.

→ **O - One Thing in the Moment**: fully focus on your actions. Tune in to your actions and the sensations you experience. Be aware of your body movements while walking, cleaning, or eating. Let the present moment become your sole priority.

→ **V - A Brief Vacation**: give yourself a short break from the stressful situation. Step outside for a brief walk, enjoy your favourite coffee or smooth, read a magazine or newspaper, or disconnect from technology. Take time to relax.

→ **E - Self-Encouragement** and Rethinking the Situation:
1. Encourage yourself with positive thoughts.
2. Repeat supportive phrases to yourself, such as "I can handle this," "This situation won't last forever," and "I'm doing my best."
3. Rethink the event from different perspectives and seek alternatives or solutions.

Use these IMPROVE strategies when faced with a stressful or crisis. Experiment with each to discover which ones help you enhance the moment and effectively manage difficulties.

Remember that improving the present moment requires practice and dedication, but it can positively impact your resilience and overall well-being.

EXERCISE 28:
Find Your Way

⏱ 15 mins

This exercise invites you to explore your creativity and problem-solving skills. You will be engaged in a virtual adventure where you must find your way through a complex path, solving puzzles and overcoming obstacles. The objective of the exercise is not only to have fun but also to develop your critical thinking, concentration, and perseverance.

② Imagine yourself in a magical, mysterious place with roads, paths, and intersections. Each route represents a choice you have to make in your real life.

Start exploring this world by taking a virtual walk through the enchanting landscape. Pay attention to details such as the colours, sounds, and smells surrounding you. Try to immerse yourself in the experience fully.

③

④ Along the way, you encounter the following puzzles to solve and obstacles to overcome. Try to solve them creatively and innovatively:

① Imagine being immersed in an imaginary world full of mysteries and challenges. Visualize this world in your mind and imagine yourself as the protagonist of an epic adventure.

FIND YOUR WAY • THINK UNLIMITED ↑

The Door Riddle: you come across three doors: a red one, a blue one, and a green one. Above each entry, there is a sign, but only one of them is correct. The sign above the red door says, "Your destination is behind this door." The sign above the blue door says, "The correct door is the green one." The sign above the green door says, "The correct door is not the red one." Which door should you choose?

The Key Riddle: You come across a closed door, and you have three different keys. Above each key, there is a word: "Truth," "Wisdom," and "Courage." Only one of these keys opens the door. Which key should you choose?

The Animal Riddle: You encounter the silhouette of a mysterious animal along the path. You are told that the animal has four legs and a long neck. It is neither a dog nor a giraffe. What is the mysterious animal?

⑤ Whenever you encounter an obstacle or difficulty, please take a moment to reflect on how to face it in real life. Ask yourself what skills or resources you possess that could help you overcome the obstacles and find the best solution.

⑥ At the end of the journey, ask yourself what lessons you have learned and how to apply them to your life. Also, consider the skills you have developed through the exercise, such as creativity, perseverance, and problem-solving ability.

This exercise allows you to explore the concept of finding your path in life, facing challenges, and making decisions. This virtual adventure inspires you to be more aware of your choices and tackle challenges with determination and creativity.

SAILING THROUGH REALITY

Open your eyes and embrace reality! **Reality acceptance** skills are the key to freeing yourself from suffering and finding inner freedom. There is no need to hide or fight against the life you have, but rather learn to dance with it. Get ready to discover the skills that will guide you towards more significant serenity and fulfilment:

- ➲ **Awaken your awareness**. Imagine wearing the glasses of understanding. Tune into the present moment and embrace everything life offers you without judgment. Discover the beauty that lies in the small things.

- ➲ **Face your thoughts and feelings**. Acknowledge that thoughts are just words in your mind and emotions are like waves that come and go. Observe them with curiosity and kindness without trying to change or judge them.

- ➲ **Let go of the struggle** with the ideal image. Break the chains of illusion and stop comparing your life to an idealized image. Embrace reality as it is and find its authentic value.

- ➲ **Feed your heart** with kindness. You must be your own best supporter, offering yourself kindness and compassion. Permit yourself to experience all emotions, welcoming your being with unconditional love.

Reality acceptance is an abstract idea and an inner journey that allows you to embrace your life in all its magnificent complexity.

ACCEPTING REALITY

Radical Acceptance is the key to breaking free from unhappiness and finding deep peace. It is the brave act of embracing the reality of life as it is, without resistance or combat. It is not about blind approval or passivity but rather a fearless awareness that allows us to release the burden of bitterness and the struggle against reality.

Reality is what it is, yet we often strive to change it or cling to a distorted idea of how it should be. Accepting Reality teaches us that rejecting reality amplifies our pain and traps us in a cycle of suffering. Only by taking the truth of the facts, even when they are painful, can we begin to transform our experience.

Every event has a cause, and every situation, even the one that causes pain, can teach us something. Accepting Reality reminds us that we cannot avoid pain but can choose how to respond. When we embrace reality without resistance, we find the calm that opens us up to the possibility of living a meaningful life despite adversity.

Accepting Reality is the way out of the hell of unhappiness. Through this sadness, we open the door to a more authentic and fulfilling life. Rejecting to accept the misery that is the way out of hell condemns us to remain trapped in the cycle of pain and suffering. Challenge yourself to practice the acceptance of reality in your daily life. Dare to accept the fact as it is without trying to change it or resist it. Only then can you discover the inner freedom and peace you yearn for.

Remember, Accepting Reality gives you the strength to accept reality and find a way to move beyond it. It is the first step towards a more authentic life.

EXERCISE 29:

Riding The Waves

10 mins

Get ready for an exciting adventure in the <u>ocean of acceptance</u>, where you will learn to navigate the waves of reality. Follow the instructions to begin your journey towards greater acceptance.

1 Imagine yourself on the beach. Find a peaceful spot where you can relax. Picture yourself on a beautiful beach, with crashing waves and the sea breeze gently caressing your face. Visualize this scene in your mind, diving into the <u>feeling of peace and calm</u>.

2 Look at the waves of <u>acceptance</u>. Fix your gaze on the imaginary ocean in front of you. Each wave represents an aspect of reality that you are seeking to accept. Observe the different shapes and sizes of the waves, recognizing that each wave represents a challenge, a change, or a fact of life.

3 Face the waves with <u>Mindfulness</u>. Choose a wave that you wish to compare and dive into the experience. Take deep breaths and let the wave reach you. As the wave envelops you, look at your reactions and emerging emotions. Acknowledge that reality is what it is and that you cannot change it, but you can change your response.

4 Float on the wave of acceptance. Imagine surrendering to the wave, carrying yourself by its strength. Fully accept the reality that the wave stands for <u>without judgment or resistance</u>. Feel the fluid movement of the wave supporting you, gently guiding you towards greater acceptance.

5 Repeat with other waves facing different challenges or aspects of reality you wish to accept. Notice how you feel as you <u>surrender to the waves</u> and how your perspective may shift as you allow yourself to be carried by the stream of acceptance.

Final remark.

After facing several <u>waves of acceptance</u>, take some time to reflect on your journey. Write down your reflections on how you felt during the exercise, what you have learned about your ability to accept reality, and how you can apply this awareness in your daily life.

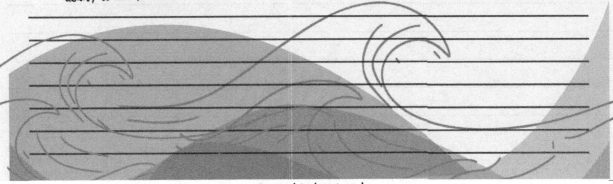

CROSSROAD

In this journey of personal growth, we will explore the power of mental transformation and the importance of accepting the reality surrounding us. The human mind is a powerful tool that can deeply influence our emotional well-being and our ability to face life's challenges.

Often, we face events that seem unacceptable or cause us suffering. However, turning one's mind means making a conscious choice to accept reality as it is instead of resisting or denying it. This doesn't mean we have to approve or be passive in the face of troubles, but rather that we must acknowledge what is beyond our control and find a way to address it constructively.

Imagine your mind at a crossroads, with one path leading to the rejection of reality and another leading to acceptance. Through this exercise, we will learn to turn our minds towards the path of acceptance, leaving away from the direction of rejection and resistance. It is a process that requires commitment and perseverance, but it will lead us towards greater inner peace and better management of life's challenges.

Remember that the choice to accept does not automatically entail a definitive acceptance. It is an ongoing journey where we commit to making this choice again and again over time.

_____

_____

_____

_____

_____

_____

_____

_____

_____

_____

_____

_____

_____

_____

_____

EXERCISE 30:
The Right Path

10 mins

Get ready to embark on a journey of mental transformation, where you will learn to make conscious choices towards acceptance. Follow the instructions to begin your path towards an open and flexible mind.

5 Practice acceptance

every day. Observe situations where you might experience resistance or a desire to deny reality. Consciously accept and allow your mind to adapt to this more open perspective.

Creative

Thinking

1 Close your eyes and

Close your eyes and visualize an imaginary crossroad in your mind. Imagine two roads branching out in front of you. One represents the path of acceptance, and the other represents the path of rejecting reality.

2 carefully read the

mental signs placed along both roads. On the path of acceptance, the characters display words like "openness," "understanding," and "change," while on the path of rejecting reality, the terms are "resistance," "denial," and "stubbornness."

4 During the journey

you may face mental obstacles that try to turn you away from the path of acceptance. Recognize these thoughts of resistance or denial and let them go. Resume your journey towards acceptance.

REALITY
REALITY
REALITY

3 Take a mindful decision

and choose to take the path of acceptance. Visualize yourself starting to walk on this path, feeling your mind open up to the possibility of accepting reality as it is.

Write down your reflections on how you felt during the exercise, what you have learned about your ability to transform the mind through acceptance, and how you can apply this awareness in your daily life.

_____
_____
_____
_____
_____

A POWERFUL QUALITY

Willpower allows us to respond to life's challenges with wisdom, openness, and without grudges. It is the ability to fully present and engage in our experiences and accept life's opportunities.

Often, we find ourselves in situations that require a choice: we can be stubborn and resist change or accept the willingness to adapt and grow. Willpower is the opposite of stubbornness, enabling us to embrace challenges and respond constructively without being trapped in the past or holding grudges.

The Master Your Mind exercise invites us to explore our willingness to enter life and actively participate in it fully. It is an invitation to become aware of our choices, to explore new opportunities, and to live with intention. It is a journey of personal growth that urges us to overcome our resistance and embrace change with fearlessness and confidence.

You will be called upon to practice willpower in many ways. You will be asked to respond to situations with wisdom, adopt an open mindset, and let go of resentment. You will be invited to experience the joy of fully participating in life, embracing challenges as opportunities for growth, and discovering the potential that lies within you.

It is time to explore the powerful force of willpower and embrace the opportunity to thrive and prosper in life.

_____

_____

_____

_____

_____

_____

_____

_____

_____

_____

_____

_____

_____

_____

_____

EXERCISE 31:
Master Your Mind

The exercise aims to develop an awareness of the difference between willpower and stubbornness, learning to recognize the clues that indicate when we are clinging to stubbornness.

1
Take a moment to reflect on situations in which you have experienced stubbornness. What extreme thoughts or phrases did you have, such as "It's impossible!" or "I can't do it!"? Please take note of these phrases or thoughts and write them down on a piece of paper.

2
Take care of the signals that indicate when you are becoming stubborn. Pay attention to your thoughts, reactions, and emotions throughout the day. When you notice extreme or rigid thoughts like the ones you identified in the previous step, pause for a moment, and become aware of what is happening. Record these moments of stubbornness on the paper.

3
Now, let's move on to the practical exercise to develop willpower. Choose an activity or challenge that requires personal commitment. It could be something you have been putting off, a fear you want to face, or a goal you want to achieve. Make a conscious decision: approach this challenge with willpower, commitment, and an open mind.

4
Take a moment to reflect While engaged in the activity, observe your thoughts and emotions. If you notice signs of stubbornness arising, such as extreme or rigid thoughts, take note of them but try not to hold onto them. Remember the goal of developing willpower and keep an open mind.

7
When challenges or obstacles arise, try to adapt, and find alternative solutions. Maintain an open and flexible perspective, avoiding closing yourself off to stubbornness. Complete the activity or challenge with steadfast commitment. Focus on the process and your attitude, striving to maintain a firm and open will.

6
After completing the activity, take some time to reflect on your willpower process. Write down your observations, the challenges you faced, and the emotions you experienced along the way. Notice if you have experienced a sense of openness, flexibility, and willingness to adapt to the situation.

5
Go on practising the "Master Your Mind" exercise in other areas of your life, approaching challenges with willpower and commitment. Over time, you will develop a greater awareness of the difference between willpower and stubbornness, learning to let go of stubbornness and embrace the mental flexibility and openness necessary for transformation.

Remember that willpower is an ongoing process, so be kind to yourself. Experiment, learn, and grow through the exploration of your mind and the mastery of will.

_____
_____
_____
_____

BE KIND TO YOUR MIND

SMILING AND OPEN

Accepting reality can occur not only mentally but also physically. I want to discuss two practices that can help you accept reality with your body.

Smiling

Relax your face. Let go of every facial muscle from the top of your head to your chin and jaw. Relax your forehead, eyes, and eyebrows; let go of your cheeks, mouth, and tongue; keep your teeth slightly apart. If you find it challenging, try tensing the facial muscles and then releasing them. Slightly lift the corners of your lips. Feel your lips lift somewhat so that you can perceive the change. This **half-smile** may be invisible to others, but you will feel a peaceful expression. Remember that your face communicates with the brain, and your body connects to the mind.

Open

Choose the best position for you.

- ☞ **Standing**. Imagine lifting your arms slightly towards the sky, creating an open, welcoming space. Your hands are relaxed, fingers stretching out like delicate leaves outward. As you do this, brush your lips with a half-smile, conveying a sense of openness and acceptance of reality. Feel the energy flow through your hands and the warmth of the smile spreading throughout your being.

- ☞ **Sitting**. Gently place your hands on your thighs as if holding a precious treasure. Your hands are open, palms facing upward, ready to receive what life offers you. As you do this, let a half-smile illuminate your face, manifesting your willingness to accept reality with openness and joy. Feel the serenity spreading through your hands and the warmth of the smile spreading into your heart.

- ☞ **Lying down**. Relax your arms by your sides, letting your body unwind in total serenity. Your hands are open, palms facing upward like the petals of a flower opening. As you do this, let a half-smile brighten your face, radiating radical acceptance in every part of you. Feel a sense of peace enveloping your hands and the warmth of the smile spreading throughout your being. Find a quiet place to dedicate a few minutes to practising the half-smile and adopting your preferred position. Focus on relaxing your face and the sensations in your hands as you become aware of your body.

Reflect on how these practices influence your ability to accept reality. Note the sensations, emotions, and thoughts you experience during the exercise.
Continue to explore and experience these practices of physical acceptance, integrating them into your daily routine.

Remember that the body and mind are closely connected; accepting reality can begin with small gestures and positions.

EXERCISE 32:
Mercy

In this exercise, we will

practice the art of a compassionate smile and openness as we reflect on a person who may have given pain or with whom we have difficulty. Through this practice, we will seek to cultivate compassion and free ourselves from anger and grudge. Are you ready? Take a comfortable position and prepare to explore new inner horizons.

10 min

1

Focus on your breath.
Take deep and relaxing breaths.. Allow yourself a _half-smile_, letting your lips lift gently. This inner smile represents the willingness to embrace compassion in your heart.

Thank You!

2

Place your hands open on your knees or in your lap, palms facing upward. Feel the energy flow through your hands, ready to transmit compassion and acceptance. Visualize the image of the person who has caused you suffering or with whom you have difficulty. Keep in mind the characteristics that bother you or find unpleasant.

3

Take time to examine what might bring happiness to this person and what might cause suffering in their daily life. Seek to understand their experiences and the challenges they may face. Observe this person's perceptions and perspectives. Try to put yourself in their shoes and understand their patterns of thought and reasoning. Explore what justifies this person's hopes and actions. Try to see their ambitions and deep desires.

4

Finally, reflect on this person's self-awareness. Notice if their opinions and insights are open and accessible or may be influenced by biases, narrow-mindedness, hatred, or anger. Observe if this person can consciously make decisions and manage their emotions.

5

Continue to explore these remarks until you feel compassion rise in your heart like a well filled with fresh water. Let anger and resentment dissolve, replaced by compassion, and understanding.

Practice this exercise multiple times on the same person, allowing compassion to grow within your being. Remember that this exercise takes time and patience but can lead to deep inner transformation.

MINDFULNESS OF THOUGHTS

Awareness of Thoughts allows us to cultivate a healthy and non-judgmental relationship with our thoughts.

When it comes to our thoughts, we often identify so strongly with them that we create a fusion between our identity and the beliefs themselves. This can lead to challenges, such as self-criticism, anxiety, and a sense of being "trapped" in our thought patterns.

Awareness of Current Thoughts invites us to develop a different relationship with our thoughts, observing them with kindness, without judgment, and without the need to act upon them. Becoming aware of our current thoughts allows us to separate the observer from the thought itself, bringing greater clarity and freedom to our mental experience.

In the following exercise, we will be guided through a process of awareness of current thoughts. Through patient observation and gentle recognition of our thoughts, we will develop the ability to be here and now without being enslaved by our thoughts.

_____

_____

_____

_____

_____

_____

_____

_____

_____

_____

_____

_____

_____

_____

_____

_____

_____

_____

_____

EXERCISE 33:
The Lightness of Being

10 mins

You are about to experience the balance between your thoughts, emotions, and body. Begin by focusing on your breath, becoming aware of the flow of air entering and leaving your body. Allow yourself to relax and let go of any tension, opening your mind to the present moment.

1

Imagine your thoughts as colourful acrobats balancing a tightrope suspended in the void. Visualize these thoughts as fascinating figures dancing and moving on your delicate balance line. Observe the different shapes and various colours that represent your thoughts.

2

Now, envision yourself as the master of balance, holding a long, flexible staff. With concentration and grace, move your team to balance your thoughts. With each movement of the staff, you will notice that the thoughts harmonize, become calmer, and float more gracefully.

3

As you continue to skilfully move the staff, experience the sensation of control and awareness of your thoughts. Observe how the balance of your thoughts influences your mood and overall well-being. You can explore different positions or movements of the staff, allowing your creativity to guide the process.

4

During this exercise, you may notice that some thoughts are more challenging to balance. Accept that balance may take time and practice. Remember that you are the master of balance and can find stability and harmony within your mind.

Conclude the exercise by returning to your breath, feeling the energy spreading throughout your body. Carry this awareness throughout your day, knowing you can return to the art of balance whenever you wish.

Chapter 5: Words Matter

INTERPERSONAL EFFECTIVENESS

In this chapter, we will explore the **social and relational skills** of DBT for teens, which play a fundamental role in building healthy relationships, managing interpersonal conflicts, and effectively achieving our goals.

Interpersonal effectiveness skills help us develop new relationships, strengthen existing ones, and handle conflict situations. These skills teach us to express our desires effectively, ask for what we want, and say no to unwanted requests while respecting ourselves and others.

In the context of DBT, interpersonal effectiveness skills are divided into <u>three main groups</u>:

- ♦ **Getting What You Want** with Skill. We will learn how to get what we want from others while maintaining healthy relationships and respecting our values.

- ♦ **Building and Ending Destructive Relationships**. We will explore how to find positive friendships, nurture meaningful relationships, and recognize when it's necessary to end relationships that are harmful to our well-being.

- ♦ **Walking the Middle Path** Skills. We will discover how to balance acceptance and change in relationships, learn to manage differences and communicate assertively.

Effective communication is crucial in managing interpersonal conflicts and building healthy relationships. We will learn practical strategies for addressing differences of opinion, controlling anger, and resolving problems constructively.

Moreover, we will discover that there is more than one way to think about a situation. We will learn to develop mental flexibility and adopt different perspectives, thus expanding our understanding of people and the problems surrounding us.

We will also work on common issues that can arise in relationships, such as difficulty maintaining a stable relationship, the inability to get what we want, or feelings of loneliness. We will learn to overcome these challenges through relational skills and create more meaningful and fulfilling connections.

Throughout this chapter, we will explore various exercises and practical strategies that will help improve our ability to communicate mindfully, create authentic connections with others and build relationships based on mutual trust and respect.

IDENTIFYING GOALS AND PRIORITIES

GIVE

Let's explore the critical concept of setting goals and priorities in life. We will learn how to maintain and nurture healthy relationships through the **GIVE skills** (Gentle, Interested, Validate, Easy Manner). These skills will help you navigate relational challenges, communicate effectively, and harmoniously achieve your desires.

Maintaining and nurturing healthy relationships is essential for emotional well-being and balance in everyday life. The GIVE skills offer a practical approach to <u>building positive</u> and <u>fulfilling relationships</u>. Here is an overview of each skill:

- ♦ **G - Gentle**. Kindness is fundamental to establishing meaningful connections with others. You will learn to communicate respectfully, avoid judgment and criticism, and practice kindness even in complex situations.

- ♦ **I - Interested**. Being interested in others is a powerful way to establish authentic connections. It is crucial to actively listen, ask meaningful questions, and show genuine interest in others' lives.

- ♦ **V - Validate**. Validation is a crucial skill for making others feel understood and accepted. You will learn to recognize others' emotions, validate their experiences, and create a supportive and understanding environment.

- ♦ **E - Easy Manner**. Communicating simply and directly fosters open and transparent communication. You will learn to express your needs and desires assertively, avoiding aggression or passivity.

These skills will help you navigate complex relational dynamics, build healthy relationships, and achieve your goals in a balanced manner. By practising these skills, you will develop greater awareness of your relationships and gain practical tools to manage interpersonal challenges.

_____

_____

_____

_____

_____

EXERCISE 34:
One More Time

Develop the ability to <u>put yourself in others' shoes</u> and understand their emotions through creative activity.

3

Read the scene description and immerse yourself in the other character's role. Try to feel and <u>understand their emotions</u>, motivations, and perspective.

4

Once you've done that, write again the scene from the <u>other character's viewpoint</u>, highlighting the emotions and thoughts you imagined for this individual.

2

Write this scene in detail, including the characters' context, actions, and emotions. Now, imagine <u>switching roles</u> with the other person.

1

Imagine <u>being a film director</u> and thinking of an emotionally intense scene involving you and another significant person.

5

Reflect on your experience during this activity. <u>What have you learned</u> about the other character? How do they truly feel? How does your perception of the situation change?

6

Finally, consider how you can apply this new understanding in your <u>relationship with this person</u>. What can you do to be more empathetic and understanding?

This exercise will help you explore the <u>other person's perspective</u>, developing your capacity for empathy and understanding of others' emotions. Remember to maintain an open and curious attitude during the activity, allowing space for creativity and discovery.

_____

_____

_____

_____

The **DEAR MAN skills** are powerful for building healthy relationships, managing conflicts, and successfully achieving your goals.

But what does **DEAR MAN** exactly mean? Let's explore it together:

⌘ **D - Describe.** Begin by communicating clearly and precisely what you want or what is bothering you. Avoid generalizations and strive to be precise in your speech.

⌘ **E - Express.** Express your feelings, opinions, and needs directly and sincerely. Be honest about your thoughts and emotions without fear of expressing them.

⌘ **A - Assert.** Make your opinion heard and maintain a confident and respectful tone of voice. Be clear and firm in communicating what you want to achieve.

⌘ **R - Reinforce.** Highlight the potential benefits or positive consequences of accepting your requests. Emphasize how your proposal can benefit both parties involved.

⌘ **M - Mindful.** Focus on the present moment and listen carefully to the other person. Show interest and respect for their point of view, even if it may differ from yours.

⌘ **A - Appear** Confident. Demonstrate confidence and self-assurance through body language, posture, and eye contact. This reinforces your message and makes you feel more confident about your requests.

☒ **N - Negotiate.** Seek a reasonable compromise that satisfies both parties involved. Remain open to dialogue and look for solutions to create a Win-Win situation.

With these DEAR MAN skills, you can communicate effectively, build meaningful relationships, and achieve your goals.

Remember, practice makes perfect! So, challenge yourself and apply these skills in your daily interactions.

_____

_____

_____

_____

_____

_____

_____

_____

EXERCISE 35:
Listen to Me

This exercise will help you practice using the DEAR MAN skills in real life. Test your empathetic communication skills and discover how to achieve your goals assertively and respectfully.

Identify the situation. Consider a recent case where you wanted to communicate your needs or goals. Briefly describe the problem and who was involved. What did you want to achieve, or what issue did you want to address?

Describe your goals. Reflect on your specific goals in that situation. Ask yourself, "What did I want to achieve? What did I want to communicate?" Write down the objectives you had in mind, focusing on what was important to you.

Now, think about the DEAR MAN skills:

❄ Describe, Express, Assert, Reinforce, Mindful, Appear Confident, Negotiate.

❄ Choose three of these skills that are most relevant to your situation.

❄ Describe how you applied these skills in communication, providing specific examples.

Reflect on the outcome. Evaluate the result of your communication using the DEAR MAN skills. Did you achieve your goals? How was the other person's response? What did you learn from this experience? Write your reflections on communication dynamics and your active listening skills.

Future application. Take note of your learning and intentions for the future. How can you apply the DEAR MAN skills in your daily interactions? How can you improve your active listening and empathetic communication skills?

active empathy requires constant practice. Keep practising the use of DEAR MAN skills to develop successful communication.

● ● ● · · ● ● ● ● ● ● · · · ● ● ● ● ● · ·

Be kind to yourself during this learning journey and celebrate every small step forward.

NEGATIVE THOUGHTS

Let's explore the **power of negative thoughts** and how we can use our Wise Mind to manage them effectively.

Negative thoughts are like dark clouds that overshadow our state of mind. They can influence our mood, self-esteem, and perspective on life. Often, we find ourselves trapped in a whirlwind of negative thoughts that seem to take over, causing stress, anxiety, and disconnection from the present moment.

But what if I told you there is a way to approach negative thoughts wisely and mindfully? This is where the "Wise Mind" comes into play.

The **Wise Mind** is a mental state in which we are <u>balanced between reason and intuition, logic and emotion</u>. It is an experience of deep awareness where we can welcome negative thoughts without being overwhelmed.

In our daily lives, we are constantly affected by a series of negative thoughts: "I'm not good enough," "I can't do it," and "Things will never go well." These thoughts can be like a prison for our minds, not allowing us to see the opportunities and possibilities surrounding us.

But the Wise Mind teaches us to be aware of these negative thoughts, to recognize them as simple thoughts rather than definitive realities. It helps us observe the thoughts with kindness and curiosity, without judgment or identification with them.

When we cultivate the Wise Mind, we can develop the ability to experience negative thoughts without being overwhelmed by them. We can learn to <u>let them pass</u> like clouds in the sky without getting caught in an endless spiral of negativity.

Throughout this journey, we will explore strategies and techniques to cultivate the Wise Mind and deal with negative thoughts wisely and compassionately. You will discover how to practice mindfulness, reflection, self-compassion, and acceptance to transform negative thoughts into more positive and constructive ones.

_____

_____

_____

_____

_____

_____

_____

_____

_____

EXERCISE 36:
I've Got a Query

15 mins

This exercise aims to develop <u>confidence and security</u> in expressing your requests and questions effectively.

Often, we hold back from asking for what we want due to fear of rejection or the belief that it would make no difference. However, learning to ask skillfully can open up new opportunities and positive outcomes.

FYI

* Don't * GIVE UP

1 Reflect on your experience.

Think about a situation where you gave up asking for something because you believed it wouldn't make any difference. Write down the details of that situation briefly.

2 Identify the beliefs or negative thoughts

that held you back from asking. For example, you might have thought: " Asking wouldn't be worthwhile," "No matter what, I'll face rejection," or " I doubt they'll pay attention to me." Write down these beliefs.

3 Now, carefully examine the beliefs

you have identified. Ask yourself if they are valid or could be based on irrational fears or limiting past experiences. Create arguments against these beliefs and write them next to each one.

4 Take the limiting beliefs

you have examined and rewrite them more positively and empowering.
For example, "I have the right to ask for what I want" or "Asking skilfully increases my chances of getting what I want." Write down these new affirmations.

Visualization exercise

Imagine a situation where you need to ask for something you desire.
Visualize the scene as you confidently and securely express this request. Imagine a positive response and the desired outcome that follows.
Feel a sense of confidence and satisfaction in engaging in effective communication with the other person.

Choose a situation where you want to ask for something or express a question. Draw inspiration from the rewritten beliefs and positive visualization. Prepare the words you will use, focus on your inner confidence, and make your request or question with skill and confidence.

BELIEF

Final reflection. After making your request:

1. Reflect on the outcome.
2. Record your feelings while making this request and whether you noticed any change in the response or attitude of others.
3. Write down the lessons learned and how you could improve your asking ability skilfully.

Repeat this exercise with different situations and requests, gradually increasing your confidenceand competence in asking skillfully. Remember that every time you allow yourself to ask, you are opening doors to new opportunities and meaningful connections in your life.

_____

_____

_____

_____

_____

_____

_____

_____

_____

_____

_____

_____

_____

RESPECT YOURSELF

We will explore a crucial concept for our emotional and relational well-being: **self-respect**. Self-respect means communicating our desires, needs, and opinions in a fair, sincere, and value-aligned manner. The ability to do so effectively is fundamental to building healthy relationships and maintaining personal integrity.

DBT offers us valuable guidance through the "**FAST** Skills," a set of abilities that help us practice respectful firmness. Let's explore how these skills can enhance our self-respect during interactions with others.

- ☒ F - **Fair**. Being fair means considering both our needs and those of others. This involves being aware of our rights and dignity and recognizing the rights and dignity of others. We will learn to balance our self-esteem with respect for others, creating a common ground where our interactions are based on reciprocity and fair consideration.

- ☒ A - **Apologies**. Apologies are an essential part of respectful communication. We will learn to recognize when our actions have hurt others and take responsibility for our words or deeds. Sincere apologies allow us to repair damages to relationships and maintain a sense of personal integrity.

- ☒ S - **Stick to Values**. Identifying our values is essential for self-respect. We will learn to understand our priorities in life and make decisions that align with our core values. This will help us be authentic, consistent, and accurate to ourselves, contributing to our emotional well-being and respect for others.

- ☒ T - **Truthful**. It is crucial for respectful communication. We will learn to express our thoughts and feelings openly and honestly, avoiding deceit or manipulation. Being honest with others enables us to build relationships based on mutual trust and establish authenticity in how we interact with the world.

_____

_____

_____

_____

_____

_____

_____

_____

_____

_____

 **10 mins**

EXERCISE 37:
Fast

This exercise aims to improve the ability to express oneself respectfully and communicate one's desires and needs to others.

1 Imagine going back in time

and finding yourself facing that situation again. Consider how you could have expressed yourself respectfully and asked for what you wanted. Imagine yourself as a character in a video game called "The Respectful Request Challenge." Your mission is to overcome challenges and learn how to make respectful requests.

2 Take note of a recent situation

where you wished to express a desire or need but did not do so. Reflect on the reasons why you avoided making the request. Were there fears, anxieties, or uncertainties that held you back? Take note of these emotions.

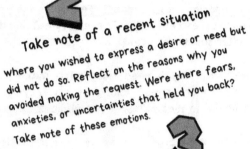

3

Create a list of "respectful skills" your character must acquire to overcome the challenges. These skills include being assertive, using respectful language, actively listening to others, and honouring your values.

4 For each skill, think of a

specific action your character could take to demonstrate that they have learned that ability. For example, you could imagine your personality making a respectful request to a friend in a video game.

5 Put yourself to the test in

the real world. Choose a situation like the one you analyzed initially and put into practice the respectful skills you identified. Try making the request you previously avoided, using the new skills you have learned.

After facing the situation, reflect on how you felt while making the respectful request. Take note of your emotions and the reactions of others.

_____

_____

_____

_____

LEARNING TO SAY "NO"

We often need help to achieve what we want. Obstacles can take different forms, such as a lack of skills, worries, intense emotions, difficulty making decisions, and external influences.

A lack of skills might make us uncertain about what to say or how to behave to get what we want. We may have the ability, but we need more self-confidence to hold us back. Worries about negative consequences may lead us to doubt ourselves and think we don't deserve what we want. We worry about not being liked by others or not meeting their expectations.

Strong emotions like anger, fear, shame, and sadness can conflict with our ability to act or communicate effectively. The emotional mind takes over and makes us say or do things that don't align with our true intentions.

At times, we might need help with making clear decisions. We find ourselves in a limbo between asking too much or not asking at all, saying "no" to everything or giving in to everything. Confusion blocks us from making conscious choices.

The environment can also influence our ability to set goals and priorities. We might feel intimidated by more powerful individuals, fear that we won't get what we need unless we sacrifice our self-esteem or worry that achieving what we want might trigger envy or dislike from others.

But fear not! This chapter will explore some strategies and skills to overcome these challenges.

You Must Know How to Say "No."

Saying "no" when necessary is an extraordinary skill! In the world of relationships and everyday interactions, the ability to express your desires and boundaries is crucial for your well-being and self-realization.

When asking for what you want, several factors must be considered. First and foremost, reflect on your priorities. How important is what you are trying to achieve? Is it related to significant goals for you? Also, consider the state of your relationship with the other person. Do you have a good rapport, or might tensions influence your request? Additionally, assess the impact on self-esteem. Does your request jeopardize your sense of worth and self-respect?

Capability is another vital aspect to consider. Are you asking for something the other person can provide? Similarly, think about whether you have something to offer in return or if you can meet the other person's needs. Timeliness is a factor to be considered. Choosing the right moment to make your request can make a difference between a positive reception and resistance.

Preparation is the key to success. Ensure you know all the relevant facts and clearly understand what you want. It is essential to explain the reason for your "no" in a practised and coherent manner. Also, consider the context of your relationship with the other person. Is it appropriate to make the request based on your relationship type?

Finally, reflect on the dynamics of giving and receiving. Has the other person helped you in the past? Do you need to set a limit because you have taken advantage of their help? Evaluate whether you have contributed in the past and if your help has been balanced.

EXERCISE 38:

Stand Strong, Say NO!

15 mins

Think about a recent event in which you felt the need to say "no" to something or someone but had difficulty doing so. It could have been an unwanted request, a commitment that didn't align with your values or a situation where you needed to defend your boundaries.

Write your response to the following questions:

Describe the situation in detail. What were you asked, or what did you need to refuse?

1 What were your feelings and thoughts in that situation? Did you feel guilty, anxious, powerless, or worried about the consequences?

2 What factors made it difficult for you to say "no"? Examples could include:
- The fear of disappointing others.
- The fear of conflict.
- The tendency to take on more responsibilities than you can handle.

3 Reflect on your values and goals. How did accepting that unwanted request or refusing to defend your boundaries align with what you consider essential?

4 Imagine how you would have felt if you had firmly said "no" in that situation. What would you have gained? How would it have affected your self-esteem and well-being?

5 Write the response you would have liked to give in that situation. Be clear, direct, and respectful. Imagine yourself saying that response. Visualize yourself confidently, maintaining your viewpoint and defending your boundaries.

6 Now, reflect on your experience and the potential positive consequences you could have obtained if you had said "no" in that situation. What would you have gained? How would it have affected how others perceive you?

Complete this exercise with sincerity. The goal is to explore how you could better handle similar situations in the future, learning to maintain your boundaries, pursue your goals, and say "no" when necessary.

Remember

that practice is essential to develop this skill. Exercise assertive communication, gradually building your confidence in saying "no" when appropriate.

Be kind to yourself and remember that you can establish your boundaries and pursue what is important to you. Stand strong, say NO!

INTEGRATING SKILLS

In the context of Dialectical Behaviour Therapy (DBT) for adolescents, this skill plays a fundamental role in achieving goals and establishing priorities in daily life. This skill focuses on the integrated synergy of various abilities and strategies to effectively address challenges and get positive outcomes.

When we talk about "abilities," we refer to the various skills learned throughout the DBT journey. These competencies include emotion regulation, stress management, assertive communication, self-awareness, and relationship skills, to name a few.

The idea of using competencies contextually entails the ability to apply and integrate these skills simultaneously during real-life situations. It means becoming aware of the different skills we have acquired and using them coherently and strategically to face the challenges that arise.

When we successfully utilize skills simultaneously, we can experience remarkable improvements in managing emotions, relationships, and everyday situations. It allows us to respond more consciously, balanced, and effectively, avoiding impulsive or unhealthy reactions. Moreover, it helps us set priorities, make more thoughtful decisions, and achieve our goals more consistently and authentically.

When reaching our goals and establishing priorities, we often need to use many skills simultaneously. Combining these abilities enables us to maximize our effectiveness and achieve meaningful results in our daily lives.

_____

_____

_____

_____

_____

_____

_____

_____

_____

_____

_____

_____

_____

_____

_____

EXERCISE 39:
Let's Have a Party

15 mins

Imagine wanting to organize a birthday party for a friend. To make this party a success, you need to apply several skills simultaneously:

Planning	You must set a date, find a suitable venue, create a guest list, and organize logistical details.	
Communication	You must inform friends about the event, send out invitations, answer questions, and keep everyone updated on the latest news.	
Time Management	You must ensure all necessary tasks are completed within the set timeframe, coordinating different tasks, and ensuring everything is ready for the party day.	
Creativity	You must create a theme for the party, decorate the venue, create fun games, and find unique ways to make the event memorable.	
Problem Solving	In the planning and execution of the party, unexpected challenges may arise. It would be best to think quickly and effectively to find appropriate solutions.	
Empathy	Consider your friend's wishes and preferences while planning the party to create a meaningful and unique experience for them.	
Self-Care	In the chaos of all the organizing, taking care of yourself, managing stress, and ensuring you have time to rest, and recharge is essential.	

Using these skills simultaneously, you can create an unforgettable birthday party that will make your friends and other guests happy. This is just one example of how the simultaneous use of various competencies can lead to success in a specific goal.

We are constantly called upon to combine our abilities to achieve our goals and establish our priorities daily. We can apply these competencies in daily activities and the more considerable challenges we face. Knowing how to use them simultaneously allows us to be more effective, face situations confidently, and achieve positive results.

OUT OF THE BOX

Are you ready to discover a new and exciting way of approaching life? We will discuss a powerful concept called "Out of the Box." This skill teaches you to go beyond standard solutions and explore innovative perspectives to overcome life's challenges.

Imagine yourself in a world where expectations and social rules seem to limit your creativity and way of thinking. Well, the "Out of the Box" thinking skill invites you to break down these mental fences and explore new ideas, original approaches, and different points of view. It drives you to think flexibly and embrace an open-mindedness that allows you to find excellent and rewarding solutions.

With this thinking skill, teenagers learn to challenge their beliefs and explore new opportunities. This will help you tackle complex situations, conflicts, and challenges that you will face along the way. You will realize that overcoming your fears and exploring new paths can lead to surprising outcomes.

We will guide you through a creative and engaging exercise to stimulate your imagination and freedom of thought. You will discover how to break free from conventional patterns and embrace an open and curious mindset.

_____

_____

_____

_____

_____

_____

_____

_____

_____

_____

_____

_____

_____

_____

_____

EXERCISE 40:
A Different View

In this exercise, we will explore the technique of REFRAMING, which involves reconsidering a situation from a different and more positive perspective. You will be guided to consider a conflict or anger-inducing situation and transform it through reframing. The ultimate goal is to develop a more <u>empathetic</u> and <u>constructive view</u> of complex situations, fostering understanding and peace in your relationships.

1   Emotions

Choose a recent situation where you experienced conflict or anger towards another person. Describe this situation briefly. Reflect on the negative emotions that this situation triggered in you.

- What are the thoughts or interpretations that fuelled these emotions?
- Record them to gain a clear understanding of how you felt.

Now, take a moment to consider a <u>different perspective</u> on this situation. Ask yourself,

- "What are the positive factors or potential opportunities I can find in this situation?" or
- "What can I learn from this experience?"

2   Reframe

Recreate the situation, trying to find <u>new meanings</u> or interpretations that allow you to see the positive or constructive side of the problem. <u>For example</u>, you could reframe a conflict as an opportunity for personal growth or learning.

Briefly describe how you reframed the situation and how <u>this</u> new point of view could influence your emotions and interactions with others. Notice if the anger subsides or you feel more open to understanding and peacefully resolving conflicts.

3   Real Life

Take a moment to reflect on how you can apply this reframing technique in other situations in your life. How can you turn hindrances into opportunities for growth and learning? How can you adopt a more empathetic and <u>constructive perspective</u> towards yourself and others?

Reframing can help you develop an open mind, better manage emotions, and promote harmonious relationships. Remember that your <u>point of view</u> can influence how you perceive and react to situations, so choose to look beyond the negative and seek the <u>bright side</u> in life's challenges.

THINK SKILLS

These skills are essential for developing an <u>empathetic and understanding perspective</u> towards others. You will learn to put yourself in the other person's shoes, consider their emotions, explore different interpretations, and notice their positive efforts. Additionally, you will be taught the importance of using kindness in your interpersonal relationships.

Thinking from the <u>other person's point of view</u> is a fundamental step in understanding their experiences and motivations. By putting yourself in their shoes, you can develop greater empathy and open-mindedness, overcoming prejudices and limiting interpretations.

<u>Generating different interpretations</u> is another crucial aspect of "Think Skills". You will challenge yourself to consider multiple explanations for the other person's behaviour, allowing for a more comprehensive and accurate view of the situation. This will help you avoid jumping to hasty conclusions or assuming that the other person's behaviour is solely motivated by negative aspects.

Noticing the <u>other person's positive efforts</u> is essential in cultivating healthy and constructive relationships. You will learn to recognize gestures of improvement, offered help, or the desire to resolve situations. At the same time, you will be encouraged to consider that the other person may be dealing with their challenges and difficulties, thus developing greater understanding and tolerance.

Finally, using <u>kindness</u> will be a valuable guide in your interactions with others. You will be invited to express yourself with gentleness, be respectful, and try to understand the needs and sensitivities of others. Using kindness will deliver an atmosphere of trust, mutual respect, and open communication.

_____

_____

_____

_____

_____

_____

_____

_____

_____

_____

_____

_____

_____

_____

EXERCISE 41:
Walking in Other Shoes

In this exercise, I challenge you to test yourself and practice your ability to <u>think</u> <u>empathetically.</u> You will have to adopt the perspective of an imaginary character and answer a series of questions about their point of view and emotions. Imagine being a young street artist performing in a funny city square. Your goal is to earn enough money to cover your daily expenses. Enter the character's mind and experience the situation as if it were your reality.

Answer the following questions, trying to understand how the character might feel:

1. What are your primary emotions while you perform? Try to identify and describe them.
2. What do you think of the audience who stop to watch your performance?
3. What would you like them to think about you?
4. Do you have expectations regarding the money you will collect?
5. What are your hopes and concerns?
6. Imagine a man who criticizes or ignores you. How do you react to this situation?
7. What might you think about that person?
8. What thoughts and feelings do you have when you see someone making a generous donation to you?
9. What would you like to express to that person?

Now, shift your perspective and imagine being one of the spectators in the square. Answer the following questions, trying to understand what you might think and feel:

1. What attracts you the most about the street artist?
2. What are your thoughts about them?
3. Are you willing to donate?
4. Why or why not?
5. How would you feel if the artist dedicated an exceptional performance to you?
6. What would you think about them?

Conclude the exercise by reflecting on your answers and comparing the two points of view.

1. What have you learned from this experience of empathetic thinking?
2. Are there differences between what you initially thought and what you experienced by putting yourself in others' shoes?

This exercise helps you <u>develop your empathy</u> and better <u>understand different perspectives.</u>

Remember that empathy is a skill that can be cultivated with constant practice. Continue exploring the emotions, thoughts, and experiences of others to broaden your understanding of the world around you.

RELATIONSHIPS WITH OTHERS

In our journey of exploring DBT therapy, we want to explore the power of words and the importance of building meaningful relationships. We will learn how to create new friendships and, at the same time, put an end to destructive ones. Communication and relationship skills are essential for growing healthy and lasting connections.

○ **Building authentic friendships.** Creating new friendships is necessary to engage and make an effort. Meaningful friendships require reciprocity and care. It is essential to remember that everyone has unique needs and desires, so try to be attentive to the needs of others. Observing, describing, and participating mindfully becomes crucial in this process.

○ **Being present and actively listening.** When you interact with others, practice the art of active listening. Indeed, be present and try to understand the emotions and thoughts of the other person. Show genuine interest and ask relevant questions to deepen the conversation. Empathy and sensitivity are keys to establishing an authentic bond with others.

○ **Recognizing and ending destructive relationships.** In addition to building new friendships, it is equally important to recognize when a relationship has become toxic or harmful. This requires courage and self-awareness. When we realize that a relationship is not benefiting us, we must make wise decisions and end it. This may take time and support, but your well-being and personal growth override.

○ **Practice authenticity and honesty.** Being authentic and expressing our feelings and needs clearly is important in building healthy relationships. You must be honest with yourself and others and balance self-respect and respect for others.

Building and maintaining meaningful relationships requires commitment and mindfulness. Using observation, description, and participation, you can make authentic and healthy connections.

Remember that every interaction is an opportunity to cultivate deep and meaningful links. Take care of your relationships and be mindful of the impact of your words on the people around you.

_____

_____

_____

_____

_____

_____

_____

_____

_____

_____

EXERCISE 42:
Get in Touch

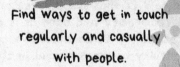

Find ways to get in touch
regularly and casually
with people.

MAKE A CHOICE

- Choose a hobby or interest that excites you and search for online groups or communities that share these passions. Actively participate in discussions and start connecting with other members.
- Explore local events or social gatherings related to topics that interest you. Attend such events and be open to new contacts.
- Look for people with similar attitudes to yours.

TELL ME YOUR VALUES

- Join groups or associations focusing on social causes or activities that reflect your values. Try to interact with people who share your visions and aspirations.
- Participate in workshops, seminars, or training courses related to topics of your interest. This will allow you to meet people who share your passions and could become friends.
- Actively engage in conversations. Offer genuine and empathetic responses to others' opinions, showing interest in what they say.

CONVERSATIONS

- Look for opportunities to participate in group conversations. Seek moments when people gather or form groups to discuss common interests. Join these conversations and share your opinions respectfully and constructively.
- Participate in online forums, discussion groups, or virtual communities of interest.

The exercise involves listing the above-described situations that the reader has already experienced or could experience. Reflecting on these opportunities and considering leveraging them to expand one's social network and build relevant relationships is essential.

WALKING THE MIDDLE PATH SKILLS

Walking the middle path is a basic skill for effectively managing oneself and relationships. This concept is based on three key abilities: dialectics, validation, and behaviour change strategies. Navigating the middle path allows us to reduce the sense of isolation, conflict, and polarity, showing the way to more balanced and fulfilling relationships.

* **Dialectics** is accepting and understanding that situations and people are often not simply "all or nothing" but exist in an intermediate zone. We recognize that things can be complex, people have different opinions, and the truth may lie in a middle ground. This dialectical stance helps us avoid extremism and seek solutions considering other perspectives.

* **Validating** the feelings, beliefs, experiences, and actions of others is relevant for building solid relationships based on trust and intimacy. It means acknowledging and respecting the emotions and viewpoints of others, even if we don't fully share them. Validation allows us to establish common ground and communicate empathically, promoting authentic and deep connections.

* **Behaviour** change strategies offer practical tools to reduce or eliminate undesirable behaviours. Extinction, for example, involves not reacting to or reinforcing inappropriate behaviour, gradually causing it to disappear. Satiation, however, requires fulfilling the underlying need that may fuel the undesirable behaviour. Finally, punishment is a targeted intervention with negative consequences to discourage inappropriate behaviour.

By consciously using these skills, we can balance our relationships, effectively manage conflicts, and promote constructive communication. Walking the middle path enables us to adopt a broader perspective, accept life's nuances, and nurture healthy and fulfilling relationships.

_____

_____

_____

_____

_____

_____

_____

_____

_____

_____

_____

_____

EXERCISE 43:
Help Yourself

Develop the ability to build a bridge between
differences. Find common ground in relationships.

UNDERSTAND

Think of a person with whom you have a relationship where there are
significant differences in interests or viewpoints.

DEFINE

Create a practical activity that helps you find common ground. Choose
a topic both of you are interested in, such as music, food, or travel.
For example, if both of you are passionate about music, organize an
evening to share your favourite playlists or play your favourite
musical instruments together.

IDEATE

Listen carefully to what they share and share your experiences and
passions on the chosen topic.
Try to maintain an attitude of mutual respect. Recognize that both of
you have valid interests and points of view. Avoid judging or criticizing the
other person's opinions and try to understand their point of view.

DISCOVER

Inquire about what the other person loves most about the chosen topic and
share what interests you. This will help create a constructive dialogue and
discover points of convergence.
At the end of the activity, reflect on the experience. Consider how your
ability to find common ground has influenced your relationship with the
other person. Have you discovered exciting new aspects of the topic? Have
you achieved a greater level of mutual understanding?

FUTURE

Plan for other future activities where you can find common ground with
the other person.
Identify new topics you are interested in and organize moments to share
your experiences and passions.

Remember:

Finding common ground requires an open mind,
curiosity, and mutual respect.

Chapter 6: Key Figures

In this chapter, we will explore the importance of key figures in an adolescent's life approaching Dialectical Behavioural Therapy (DBT): family, school, and therapist. These figures play a fundamental role in your emotional well-being and personal growth.

- **Family** is the primary social unit where you develop, learn, and grow. It is an environment where emotions are shared, challenges are faced, and lasting bonds are formed. However, every family is unique and can present complex dynamics. Some families may invalidate, punish, or deny your emotions, while others can be a source of support and comfort. This chapter will explore how to address these family dynamics and develop healthier and more meaningful relationships.

- **School** is the place where you spend a significant amount of your time, meet new people, and face academic and social challenges. School can be an exciting and rewarding experience, but it can also be a source of stress and anxiety. We will explore how to navigate school dynamics, manage stress, and develop social skills that will help you succeed academically and build positive relationships with your classmates and teachers.

- Lastly, we will talk about the **therapist**, a key figure in your personal growth journey. The therapist is there to support you, guide you, and help you develop your emotional regulation skills. They provide you with tools and strategies to cope with difficult times. Learn how to make the most of your relationship with the therapist and how to integrate the skills learned in therapy into your daily life.

Remember, this chapter aims to help you understand the important role these figures play in your life and how to interact with them. There are no perfect families, schools, or therapists, but your commitment to building healthy relationships and using the skills learned to achieve emotional well-being matters.

FAMILY

Family is a crucial element in your life and your process of growth during adolescence. Family is the social unit where you live and experience a range of emotions, thoughts, and relational dynamics that can deeply influence your emotional well-being.

Adolescence is a time of <u>intense emotions</u> and <u>extreme thoughts</u>. You may feel overwhelmed by daily challenges, struggle to handle family conflicts, or positively influence others' behaviour. These difficulties are part of the growth journey, but it is important to acquire skills that help you navigate the middle path, finding a balance between your needs and those of your family.

Often, teenagers find themselves in <u>risky situations</u> and may constantly feel uncomfortable or inadequate in social interactions. This is normal, as their brains are going through a crucial developmental phase. Over this time, their brains change and renew themselves, creating new connections and letting go of old childhood behavioural patterns to embrace more mature adult behaviours.

However, it is relevant to remember that some executive functions of the brain, such as decision-making, self-regulation, and emotional management, are not fully developed. As a result, you may experience a wide range of emotions and feelings more intensely than adults.

This transitional phase <u>determines how you will become</u> the person you want to be as an adult. It is a time when you become self-aware and aware of your relationships with others. However, for a teenager, it can be challenging to manage strong emotions such as anger, sadness, or euphoria without the proper tools to reason, assess, and take care of oneself.

In these moments, it is crucial to have an aware and authoritative adult who can listen to you, remain calm and present in the here and now, and help you understand and manage your turbulent emotions. When understanding and support are lacking in your life, suffering may manifest through behaviours that seem incomprehensible to adults.
This happens because adults often do not fully know what is happening in their minds and may not recognize the signs of distress and provide them with the tools they need to cope with the challenges of adolescence.

In DBT therapy, <u>family relationships are a key element</u> in promoting your emotional well-being. The family environment can be both a precious resource and a source of conflict. Therefore, it is important to adopt a collaborative approach and actively involve both you and your family members in managing family interactions.

Open and respectful <u>communication</u> within the family is essential. It is important to create a space where family members can express their concerns and feelings respectfully, avoiding judgment and mutual accusations.

Mutual understanding and empathy are key elements in promoting a <u>positive family atmosphere</u>.

Actively involving the family in the entire therapeutic process is an important aspect of DBT therapy. Providing information about DBT and emotional disorders, educating the family about specific dynamics, and involving them in decisions regarding the treatment path contribute to creating a collaborative and supportive environment.

DBT therapy also promotes emotional support within the family. Creating a safe space where teens can express their emotions and receive support is essential.

Another important aspect is awareness of family dynamics. Exploring specific family dynamics and identifying dysfunctional patterns or recurring conflicts can help identify factors that may contribute to the adolescent's problems. Working on these dynamics can be a significant step towards positive change.

Another crucial element is involving parents in learning DBT skills. Providing them with tools and resources to understand and support the adolescent in practising the skills learned during therapy can help create a good family environment.

Stress management is another important area of focus. Helping the family develop coping strategies for stress and daily difficulties can promote a more serene family climate. This may include relaxation techniques, time management, and promoting individual and family well-being.

Finally, collaboration with other professionals, such as family therapists or school counsellors, can be invaluable. Working in synergy with other professionals can ensure comprehensive and integrated support for teens and their families, offering a broader and more competent support network.

Every family is unique, and family involvement may vary depending on the specific needs of the adolescent and family dynamics. DBT therapy offers a framework and a set of strategies that can be customized based on individual situations.

Keep reading to explore the role of school and the therapist as key figures in your life during adolescence.

SCHOOL

The school plays a crucial role in teens lives, often becoming the place where emotional difficulties manifest. Teachers, although not therapists, play a primary educational role and, with the appropriate tools, can be of great help to all students, especially those showing signs of potential personality disorders. They can signal to the family the need for a consultation with a specialized professional.

Teachers could integrate the teaching of basics DBT skills in the school environment, providing opportunities for practice and application of the skills learned during therapy. This support in learning skills can promote emotional regulation and effective communication in adolescents, equipping them with the right tools to face daily challenges.

Collaboration between teachers and the psychotherapist is a crucial aspect. Teachers should communicate with the psychotherapist to share relevant information about the teen's progress at school and ensure consistency between the therapeutic approach and the school environment. This synergy can contribute to a more comprehensive and integrated support for the adolescent.

Creating a supportive learning environment is an important goal for teachers. They can promote awareness, emotional regulation, and effective communication within the classroom, providing appropriate tools and resources. A school environment that supports mental well-being delivers academic success and overall student comfort.

Teachers can raise awareness among students about the importance of finding a healthy balance between studies, extracurricular activities, and personal time. This awareness helps students manage stress and maintain optimal mental balance.

An inclusive approach to child and adolescent development is increasingly evident to promote long-term health. Visualizing a future with the intention of achieving it activates brain areas related to self-regulation of emotions, intentional use of memories, and self-evaluation.

Many young people feel insecure and face common age-related fears. Typical challenges of adolescence can generate tension, fear of failure, and concern about the judgment of others. Sometimes, a low grade in school or rejection from a friend can make adolescents feel uncomfortable and excluded. How they perceive themselves and their self-esteem significantly influence their behaviours.

Educators are aware of how information and images on social media can impact adolescents' self-esteem if not used consciously. Teens who are confident in their abilities and have good self-esteem are generally more prepared to face the challenges of growth. They are also better equipped to handle mistakes and turn them into opportunities to learn about themselves and others. The work on self-esteem by educators nurtures a sense of self-efficacy, influencing how adolescents define themselves, perceive themselves in the world, and relate in different life situations.

A crucial first step is self-acceptance and acceptance of one's life as an opportunity. The awareness that life itself is a gift to be grateful for allows us to look at ourselves with compassion, recognizing our strengths and flaws without exaggerating the former or denying the latter. This process involves taking responsibility for oneself and taking a step towards adulthood, where we are aware of our ability to actively engage in life.

THERAPY

The therapist's role in DBT therapy is crucial to help you in your treatment journey. The therapist is like an expert guide who assists you in understanding yourself and developing DBT skills.

One of the main tasks of the therapist is to assess and understand your situation. Through an accurate evaluation, the therapist determines if DBT is the correct therapeutic path for you. This helps establish therapeutic goals you will work on together to improve.

The professional practically teaches your DBT skills. You will learn to be mindful of yourself and your emotions, manage stress, and communicate effectively. These skills will help you healthily manage your feelings and understand how your behaviours can influence yourself and others.

The therapist provides emotional support. They will be there for you, helping you understand the challenges you face and celebrating your progress.

A relevant factor of DBT therapy concerns how you see yourself and accept yourself. The therapist helps you increase your self-esteem and learn to accept yourself for who you are. Through honest conversations, the therapist assists you in becoming more independent in managing your emotions and understanding how your behaviours can influence you.

DBT therapy manuals are often created to introduce this practice's fundamental concepts. After becoming aware of the practical help this therapy can provide the reader, it is advisable to rely on a qualified therapist who will guide you through the maze of adolescence. It is, therefore, recommended that the reader work closely with an experienced therapist to achieve the best results from DBT therapy.

Addiction

Addiction can involve various forms, such as substance addiction like alcohol or drugs, behavioural addictions like gambling, or excessive use of technological devices.

When one falls into addiction, it can seem difficult to break free and regain balance in life. Addiction can negatively impact our emotional well-being, relationships, and educational performance. It may feel like being stuck, but with the proper support and appropriate therapy, overcoming addiction and returning to living a healthy and fulfilling life is possible.

Therapy provides a safe environment where you can explore the roots of your addiction, understand what led you to develop it and learn strategies to manage it. The therapist will work with you to identify your recovery goals and develop a personalized treatment plan to help you achieve them.

Therapy may involve various approaches, so you can learn to identify and modify thoughts and behaviours that contribute to your addiction through these therapeutic modalities. You will also learn practical skills to cope with stress, intense emotions, and situations that may trigger the desire to relapse into addiction.

It is important to remember that addiction is not a personal weakness but a condition that can affect anyone. Therapy offers a supportive and understanding space, without judgment, where you can explore your experiences and learn to take care of yourself in a healthy and balanced way.

If you find yourself struggling with addiction, do not worry. With the proper support and commitment to your recovery, you can overcome this challenge and build a life filled with satisfaction.

Within DBT therapy, a specific approach is adopted to address addictions. This concept combines two important principles: abstinence, which involves a total commitment to avoiding addictive behaviour, and harm reduction, which involves planning for slips in addictive behaviour so they do not become full-blown relapses.

This concept can be likened to an Olympic athlete who, even after losing a race, continues to believe and act as if they have the potential to win every time. The approach aims to combine the motivation to achieve the highest level of success with the awareness that difficult moments and slips may occur, but they do not have to be seen as complete failures.

Adolescents learn to set goals of abstinence from the addictive behaviour while at the same time acquiring skills to anticipate and address critical situations where they may be tempted to give in to the addiction. This may include identifying triggering factors, developing alternative strategies, and engaging a support network to face challenges.

Clear Mind

"Clear Mind" is a relevant concept when discussing addictions and the role of the mind in the healing journey. It represents a balance between two extremes: the "dependent mind" and the "free mind," offering a balanced and mindful perspective.

The "**dependent mind**" represents a state entirely governed by our addiction. Urges and thoughts related to problematic behaviours take control, determining our emotions and actions. In this condition, we are driven to do anything to satisfy the addiction without considering the consequences.

On the other hand, the "**free mind**" may seem like a safe place where we think we have overcome the issues and no longer need to be on guard against a potential relapse. However, the "free mind" can lead to ignoring the dangers that could trigger problematic behaviours again. We feel invincible and immune to future temptations, putting our progress at risk.

The key to achieving a balanced and secure mind is the "Clear Mind." In this state, we know about our addiction and radically accept that a relapse is not impossible. Despite our successes, we are ready to face impulses and triggers that may test us. It is a way of living where we enjoy our achievements but are prepared to meet future temptations.

The "Clear Mind" implies a deep self-awareness and acknowledgement of our vulnerabilities. We are clean and have made significant strides in our healing, but we recognize that addiction is still a part of us. This prompts us to plan and prepare for moments when we may be tempted to fall into old habits. A sense of responsibility towards ourselves and a constant commitment to avoiding relapses remains present.

Enhancing the Environment

"Empowering the Environment" is an essential concept in the context of DBT therapy and the recovery journey from addictions. It involves restructuring the environment to support abstinence rather than dependence, creating a context that promotes a life without harmful behaviours.

Strengthening the community's defences is crucial to promote abstinence. Reinforcements in the environment play a vital role in motivating or discouraging addictive behaviours. In interrupting addictive behaviours, it is essential to understand how making a lifestyle free from such behaviours is more rewarding than one that includes them. Ways must be found to make choices that counter addictions more rewarding and appreciated by those around us. Willingness alone is not sufficient. If it were, we would all be able to avoid habits easily.

A key aspect of empowering the environment is replacing some addictive thought processes with those that promote abstinence. This involves adopting actions that increase the chances of experiencing positive events as an alternative to addictive behaviour. These actions include:

- Seek out people to **spend time with who are not involved** in addictions. Spending time with individuals who support a healthy, addiction-free lifestyle can create a positive environment.

- Increase the number of **enjoyable activities**. Explore new hobbies, sports, or interests that you are passionate about and keep you engaged healthily.

- **Explore different options**. If you are still determining the people or activities you like, try participating in groups with other people and experiment with many activities. You will discover exciting activities and people who share your values and life goals.

EXERCISE 44:
Good Habits

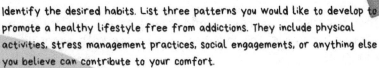

The purpose is to create an activity that helps you develop and consolidate good habits that promote a healthy lifestyle free from addictions.

Identify the desired habits. List three patterns you would like to develop to promote a healthy lifestyle free from addictions. They include physical activities, stress management practices, social engagements, or anything else you believe can contribute to your comfort.

Choose one of the identified habits and plan how you can start practising it in your daily life. For example, if you choose a physical activity, you could take a 30-minute walk every day after school or sign up for a yoga class twice a week.

Take some time to reflect on the habits you would like to develop in your life. These habits should replace problematic behaviours or addictions with positive and rewarding choices. Follow the steps below to complete the activity:

Share your new habit with a trusted person, such as a friend, family member, or teacher you trust. Ask them to support and encourage you along the way. The help and support of others can make a difference in maintaining motivation and commitment to the new habits.

Keep track of your progress in practising the new habit. Record the days you manage to follow the routine and note how it makes you feel.

Recognize and celebrate your successes along the way. For example, you can reward yourself with something enjoyable whenever you follow the habit for a week or achieve a specific goal. Rewards can be something pleasant for you, like watching a movie, walking, or spending an evening with friends.

You may need help to follow the new habit. Don't get discouraged! Reflect on what can be improved and seek new strategies to overcome the obstacles. Flexibility and adaptation are essential to maintaining good habits in the long term.

Try to be kind to yourself and appreciate the process of personal growth. Over time, the new habits will become more natural and help you live a healthy, rewarding life free from addictions.

The Bridge

Have you ever heard of the expression **"burning bridges"**? In this context, it means actively eliminating every connection to factors that can trigger addictive behaviours. It's like saying to yourself, "I will never return there again!"

Imagine having a clear and decisive vision of your path to a life free from addictions. Burning bridges allow you to make a radical decision and then take active steps to eliminate all possibilities that can fuel addiction.

Here are some steps you can take to burn bridges with addiction:

→ **Recognize the factors** that favour addiction. List all the things in your life that could facilitate addictive behaviour. This might include people with negative influences or situations that put you at risk.

→ **Eliminate temptations**. Take control and eliminate everything that could lead you back into addiction. Dispose of contact with people involved in your addiction and remove potential tricks that could push you toward the old behaviour.

→ **Don't hide behind lies** or justifications. It would be best to be honest about your past and commitment to change. Openly communicate this to your friends and family so they can support you and understand your determination to break free from addiction.

Once you've burned bridges with addiction, it's time to build new ones. This means creating new visual images and scents in your mind.

Here are some suggestions for building new bridges:

☑ **Visual images**. Try to imagine pleasant and fulfilling situations that are not related to addiction. For example, if you crave a cigarette, imagine yourself on a beautiful beach, feeling the salty air and the sun's warmth on your skin. These images can help reduce cravings and shift your focus to positive experiences.

☑ **Scents** are potent triggers for our emotions and desires. Surround yourself with pleasant scents that are not associated with your addiction. You can use perfumes, essential oils, or even simple fragrances that make you feel good. When you experience an unwanted craving, focus on these alternative scents to counter the desire.

☑ **Watch images or videos** that capture your attention and distract you from unwanted cravings. For example, you can watch videos of sports, nature, or hobbies that interest you. These images can help distance yourself from desires and focus on other experiences.

Burning bridges with addiction takes courage and commitment, but building new bridges toward a healthy, addiction-free life will allow you to explore new horizons.

EXERCISE 45:

Bridge Builder

This exercise will help you burn the old bridges with addiction and build new bridges towards a healthy and fulfilling life. Follow these simple steps to practice this exercise:

Identify your old bridges with addiction. Take a sheet of paper and list all the factors, people, or situations that can favour your addiction. This could include places, objects, people, or activities associated with addictive behaviour.

Burn the old bridges. Take another sheet of paper and write down the details of the old bridges with addiction. This could be a symbolic act of separation. Then, tear or burn the document as a symbolic gesture to free yourself from the habit. Take deep breaths and feel the sense of liberation from letting go of the past.

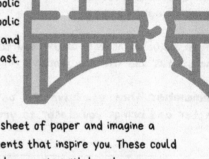

Build new positive bridges. Take a new sheet of paper and imagine a series of visual images and pleasant scents that inspire you. These could be images of relaxing landscapes, joyful moments with loved ones, or fragrances that make you feel safe and calm. Write down these images and scents on the paper, allowing them to become your new positive bridges.

Carry the new bridges with you. Cut the paper with the images and scents of your new positive bridges and keep it with you, perhaps by folding it and putting it in your wallet or a safe place. Whenever you feel the urge of addiction, touch the paper of the positive bridges, and mentally visualize the images and scents you have created. This will help you focus on the new thought patterns and strengthen your determination to follow a path of healthy living.

Joy Revolution

The "Joy Revolution" concept offers an alternative way to manage rebellion without compromising your goals and falling into the traps of addiction. Follow these suggestions to put this revolution into practice:

- ✂ **Rediscover your rebellious spirit** and drive it towards positive experiences. Instead of following the path of destructive rebellion, challenge conventions through creative, sports, or social activities that express your individuality and desire to make a difference. For example, participate in volunteering initiatives, join activist groups, or explore new forms of art that allow you to express yourself authentically and meaningfully.

Confront the belief that you desire the behaviour that leads to addiction. Challenge your negative thoughts and replace them with positive affirmations. For instance, instead of telling yourself, "I need that substance to feel good," repeat to yourself, "I can find happiness and fulfilment in healthy and rewarding ways." Train your mind to focus on life's opportunities rather than the illusion of addiction.

Challenge the monotony and dissatisfaction that can fuel the desire for destructive rebellion. Seek new adventures, discover new passions, and try to broaden your horizons. Take part in courses, cultural events, travel, or explore stimulating hobbies that allow you to experience and grow as an individual. Fill your life with meaningful and fulfilling experiences that overwhelm the need for negative behaviours.

These suggestions will allow you to improve your individuality and express your desire to challenge the status quo without jeopardizing your health.

Remember that you have the power to forge your destiny. Choose a rebellion that makes you better and brings you closer to your dreams.

_____
_____
_____
_____
_____
_____
_____
_____
_____
_____

15 mins

EXERCISE 46:
Rebel Rebel

THIS EXERCISE CHALLENGES

START HERE

you to explore your creative rebellion through an activity that allows you to embrace your individuality, challenge conventions, and promote change.

IDENTIFY YOUR REBELLION

Reflect on what makes you feel rebellious against social rules or societal expectations. It could be an opinion you want to share, a social cause you deeply care about, or an innovative idea you wish to promote. Identify your rebellion and what you want to express through your creativity.

CHOOSE YOUR WAY OF EXPRESSION

Every form of art can be a powerful vehicle to express your creative rebellion. Choose the form of expression that inspires you the most: writing, music, painting, dance, photography, or any other form of art that allows you to convey your message authentically and engagingly.

REFLECT ON THE EFFECT YOUR REBELLION HAS ON PEOPLE EXPERIENCING IT

Look at the reactions, discussions that arise, and potential actions that may occur from your message. Use this inspiration to fuel your creative rebellion further and turn it into concrete action for the change you wish to see in the world.

BRING YOUR REBELLIOUS PROJECT TO THE PUBLIC
Organize an event where you can showcase your artwork or share your performance with others.
Invite friends, family, and people who share your vision to participate and support your creative rebellion.

Whether writing a musical piece, painting a picture, or creating a video, do it passionately and without fear of breaking conventions. Express your unique vision through your project, using symbols, colours, texts, or movements representing your creative rebellion.

PUT YOUR CREATIVITY INTO ACTION AND BRING YOUR REBELLIOUS PROJECT TO LIFE

Remember

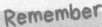

Your creative rebellion is an opportunity to express your individuality, promote change, and leave your mark on the world. Accept your authenticity and be brave in putting your creative rebellion into practice. Your message and creativity can make a difference!

Dear Reader,

To enhance your experience, we've prepared **Three More Assets**!

Use this code to download these gifts for free.

View, write down and organize.... want to know more about these tasks? Use the code with your smartphone or tablet; it will take you directly to the right page.

Your **Feedback** is crucial to me.
If you found this book helpful or inspiring, please consider leaving your opinion. It will help other readers discover this resource and help me create more valuable content for teens like you.

Leaving a comment is quick and easy. 1) Use the code with your smartphone or tablet, point your camera to take you directly to the right page 2) From Amazon.com/book page, scroll down to the "Customer Review" section. Click on "Write a customer review" Choose your star rating, share your honest and genuine thoughts, and click submit.

Exercise 9:
Answers: 1 – a, 2 - b, 3 - b, 4 – c, 5 - b

Conclusion

Dear reader,
You have completed an incredible journey through the "DBT Workbook for Teens" that has led you to discover yourself, your emotions, and your potential. You have learned valuable life skills that will help you face challenges and grow as an individual.

On this journey, you have explored the **key figures** fundamental to your healing path. You have discovered how family can be a valuable support network, the school can offer you opportunities for learning and growth, and therapists can lead you towards positive change. You have understood the importance of cultivating a healthy, empowering, and addiction-free environment.

Now you have basic skills to **explore powerful concepts** such as mindfulness, self-acceptance, emotional management, and building meaningful relationships. You have learned to recognize your thoughts, explore your emotions, and communicate effectively. You have discovered that you can create your future, overcome fences, and embrace your uniqueness.

You can grow, learn, and discover **new aspects of yourself** every day. If you stumble along the way, keep going. Every fall is an opportunity to rise stronger than before.

Remember to always **take care of yourself**. Seek the support of people who love and help you. Forgive your mistakes and celebrate your successes, big and small. Continue to apply your learned skills, experience new things, and follow your passions.

Your story is unique and precious. Never stop dreaming, believe in yourself, and follow what makes you feel alive.

Good luck. The world is ready to welcome your magnificent contribution.

With love and hope,

Erin Parker

FAQs (Frequently Asked Questions)

1. What is DBT (Dialectical Behaviour Therapy), and how can it help me as a teenager?

DBT (Dialectical Behaviour Therapy) is a therapeutic approach developed by psychologist **Marsha M. Linehan**. She designed it to help individuals struggling with emotional instability and complex relationships. It is shaped to help people develop skills in emotional regulation, stress management, improved interpersonal relationships, and self-awareness. DBT is particularly beneficial for teenagers because it provides practical tools to address the emotional, behavioural, and relational challenges that arise during this stage of life.

DBT focuses on developing <u>specific skills</u>, such as recognizing and regulating intense emotions, managing conflict in relationships, effective communication, and self-awareness. These skills help teenagers develop a sense of emotional balance, make informed decisions, and establish healthier relationships with others.

DBT utilizes strategies, including teaching skills, emotional support, and creating a safe therapeutic environment. Through regular practice of DBT skills, teenagers can <u>learn to manage their emotional</u> states better, make more informed decisions, and build more positive and fulfilling relationships.

DBT can help you as a teenager by providing the tools to effectively cope with life's challenges, healthily manage your emotions, and build meaningful relationships. This journey allows you to grow, develop self-awareness, and achieve lasting mental and emotional well-being.

2. What is the difference between this book and other books on DBT therapy?

The "DBT Workbook for Teens" stands out from other books on DBT therapy for several reasons. Firstly, it has been designed for teenagers, considering their unique needs, challenges, and interests. This means that the book is written in an <u>accessible language</u> and <u>age-appropriate manner</u>, making it easier for teenagers to understand and apply the concepts of DBT.

Furthermore, it is structured as an actual workbook, offering practical exercises, interactive activities, and spaces for personal writing. This interactive and engaging approach allows teenagers to apply DBT skills directly in their daily lives, encouraging active learning and personal transformation.

Finally, the "DBT Workbook for Teens" provides a wide range of tools and resources for support. In addition to exercises and activities, the book offers practical tips, strategies, and helpful advice for tackling daily challenges. Moreover, it can be an introductory tool for teens to reflect on their challenges and complement DBT therapy sessions with a professional.

In summary, the "DBT Workbook for Teens" stands out for its adaptability to teenagers, interactive structure, attention to their specific experiences, and a wide array of practical tools it offers. It is a valuable resource for teenagers seeking to explore DBT therapy effectively and meaningfully.

3. What age should you be to benefit from the "DBT Workbook for Teens"?

It is designed for adolescents between the **ages of 13 and 19**. This age range is significant as it corresponds to a crucial developmental stage in which many teens may face emotional, relational, and behavioural challenges.

However, it is essential to emphasize that everyone may benefit from the workbook, even outside of this age range. Depending on their specific needs and experiences, some younger or older teenagers may find the material helpful.

Lastly, it is crucial to highlight that the "DBT Workbook for Teens" can be read independently. This allows teenagers to reflect on their challenges and provides complementary support to DBT therapy sessions with a professional. In either case, the involvement and support of parents or a trusted adult can greatly help teenagers use the workbook and apply DBT skills in their daily lives.

In summary, the ideal age to benefit from the "book is between 13 and 19 years old, but every individual may find the material helpful regardless of age. It is important to consider each teenager's emotional and cognitive maturity and involve the support of parents or trusted adults while using the book.

4. *Can I use the book independently, or need a therapist to guide me?*

The workbook is a valuable tool for gaining an initial understanding of DBT therapy and starting to work on the skills and strategies shown in the book. It can be read and used on your own as an initial guide.

However, it is essential to emphasize that involving a qualified adult, such as a teacher or therapist, can offer numerous advantages in your journey of growth and change. These professionals have specific expertise in DBT therapy and can help you apply the skills more effectively by providing targeted feedback and personalized guidance.

A qualified teacher or therapist can more accurately identify your needs and work with you to address specific issues or challenges you may face. They can provide an external perspective, offer emotional support, and help you integrate DBT skills into your daily life more effectively.

So, even though you can start working on the "DBT Workbook for Teens" on your own, we always recommend involving a qualified adult with specific DBT expertise to accompany you on this journey. This can ensure greater support, personalized guidance, and a better understanding of your needs.

5. *Can I use the workbook along with other forms of therapy or treatment?*

The book can be a complementary tool to help you develop and practice emotional regulation, stress management, effective communication, and self-awareness skills, which are universally valuable competencies.

You can integrate the work with the book into your journey if you are already attending specific therapy or treatment. However, discussing your intentions with your therapist or counsellor to explore ways to effectively combine the strategies and skills learned in the book with other therapies or treatments is essential.

Remember that mental health is an individual journey, and different approaches can be considered. The key is communicating openly with your healthcare provider and working together to create a personalized plan that suits your specific needs.

The book can provide valuable tools for your emotional well-being, but it's always advisable to work alongside a qualified professional who can guide and support you on your path. Combining different forms of therapy can offer a comprehensive approach to addressing your challenges.

Made in the USA
Columbia, SC
05 December 2024

48499373R00070